don rogers

the authorised biography

don rogers
the authorised biography

PETER MATTHEWS

TEMPUS

To my grandparents, Swindonians all, who watched Don on a regular basis, with thanks for all their love and support in my early years.

First published 2004

Tempus Publishing Limited
The Mill, Brimscombe Port,
Stroud, Gloucestershire, GL5 2QG
www.tempus-publishing.com

British Library Cataloguing in Publication Data.
A catalogue record for this book is available from the British Library.

ISBN 0 7524 3293 1

Typesetting and origination by Tempus Publishing Limited
Printed and bound in Great Britain

Contents

Acknowledgements

Any book is a team effort, and this one is no different. So many people have given generously of their time to help me out that the list seems endless. Let me try personally to thank everybody.

Firstly, my thanks to Mike Judd and Podge Rodgers. Without them, the book may never have existed, and they have both given advice and help as the book has developed – Mike has been helpful in introducing me to people at Swindon, and Podge's cheery phone calls have kept me going when there has seemed much to do.

James Howarth at Tempus put us all together and has, as with my previous books, been very helpful. Huge thanks too to Mike's son, Nick Judd, who has been my chief researcher – getting hold of old pictures and match reports in his own free time. Two longstanding Swindon fans, Dave Wallis and Roy Ferris, also lent me material that was of enormous help. My dad was an excellent proofreader and, as someone who saw many of Don's greatest games, gave me useful background information.

Clive Bettison, for many years secretary of Lambourn Sports (the first club Don managed), not only gave me his views on Don's time there, but also lent me a large scrapbook containing many match reports and features relating to Don's career, which was hugely useful in providing some contemporaneous material for the book.

The Swindon Town historian Dick Mattick has been exceptionally generous with the loan and sharing of his priceless material on the club, and has shown no concern that I have entered 'his patch' – quite the reverse in fact. His books on Swindon set the standard for the history of the club, and I wish him well with his own book on the club's greatest matches, due out this winter. The Reverend Nigel Sands, the official historian of Crystal Palace, was also very helpful in putting Don's spell at Selhurst Park in context.

This book is an authorised biography – that is to say it is written with Don's full co-operation and support. Much of the book contains his own reflections on his career, but to get the views of other people I have spent time talking to several of his former teammates, most notably John Trollope, Keith Morgan, Rod Thomas, Frank Burrows, Bruce Walker and Alan Whittle. All have given freely of their time and again I am very grateful.

Finally, to Don, and his family, my thanks. Don could not have been more helpful in the writing of this book, and was open and honest about his career in the game, as well as lending me some of his own mementoes. I trust the book does justice to a genuine man, and a great footballer.

Introduction

For a club that has spent much of its near-125 years of existence predominantly in the lower two leagues of English football, provincial Swindon Town has been fortunate in having some great players grace its doors. Don Rogers, for a combination of what he did for the club over a period of time, together with the sheer excitement he brought to the game, was surely the greatest of them.

There are, of course, other contenders. Harold Fleming (a cousin of my paternal grandfather cousin, in case you are interested) played for England while Swindon were still a non-League club and inspired some great cup runs in the early 1900s. Harry Morris scored goals for fun in the 1930s. John Trollope set a record for League appearances for one club that will probably never be beaten.

The County Ground, home of the club (for the present, anyway) has also seen great players at the start and end of their careers. In the former category would sit Mike Summerbee, who went on to great things with Manchester City, and Ernie Hunt, who will forever be immortalised for that 'donkey flip' goal while playing for Coventry. Both, as contemporaries of Don, feature in this book. In the latter category of veterans would sit more recent players, such as Lou Macari, Ossie Ardiles and Glenn Hoddle – all player-managers of the club. Macari and Ardiles, great players though they were, rarely actually took to the pitch for the club; Hoddle was different – two seasons in the early 1990s of watching one of England's most gifted footballers spraying the ball around the pitch was a fantastic experience.

Despite such competition, Don would get my, and a lot of other people's vote, for a number of reasons. Firstly, he was such an exciting player to watch. It is difficult to convey just how exhilarating a sight he was, thirty years on – but some of the contemporary match reports (I hope) go some way to doing this. In an era where football had more 'entertainers' than today, he was the commensurate performer – as one Swindon fan of the 1960s said: 'We went to watch him, not the team.'

Secondly, Don was not just an entertainer; he was a goalscorer as well. If you look at the records of some of the other wingers of that time, they simply do not stand up to comparison with Don's. He didn't just make goals, he scored them too: 148 for Swindon alone, not to mention the goals at his other clubs. He remains Swindon's third-highest goalscorer of all time. Not bad for a man who was supposed to be on the wing.

Thirdly, he inspired the club to success they could only previously have dreamt of. Don's first spell at the club, 1962 to 1972, saw what was a ramshackle Third Division club transformed into, for a spell, one of the best sides outside the First Division. Of course, it wasn't just Don, but somehow he was the talisman and the man whom most fans outside of Wiltshire associated with the club.

Fourthly, 15 March 1969: the club's greatest ever day. Need I say more?

Finally, and perhaps this is key, Don also performed on the highest stage. True, it was only briefly, but for one fleeting half-season, he was centre stage, as one of the top players in English football. Indeed, during that season of 1972/73, one rival manager, after seeing Don tear his side apart, described him as 'the best footballer in England'. It says much for Don that he is remembered almost as fondly at Crystal Palace as he is in Wiltshire. He showed that he could be just as influential in the First Division as the Second or Third. It is the one tragedy of this story that he never got the chance to play at the highest level consistently, or arguably, early enough.

The idea for this book came in the summer of 2003, when I visited Don at his sports shop in the town where he made his name. Don was interested, but was tied up with work at the shop; I was then busy with other projects, and it wasn't until the beginning of 2004 that I made contact again. Then I got the news that Don had decided to do the book, but as he hadn't heard from me, he had decided to go with 'somebody from the club' who had approached him over the Christmas break. Kicking myself for not having phoned sooner, I wished Don all the best with the book, and put the phone down,

Four days later, the phone rang. It was James Howarth from Tempus to say that he had been approached by some people who wanted to do a book on Don, but needed someone to write it. Would I be interested? This time I prevaricated not, met up with Mike Judd and Podge Rodgers – Don's friends from 'the club' and who would both become good friends during the writing of the book – and the project was underway.

So why me to write the story of Don? Some context is needed. They say that you never forget the first time you saw a football match – the noise, the excitement, the crowd, being passed down to the front so you could see properly, all that kind of stuff. Well I am the exception to that rule. Although both my parents were from Swindon, and along with their parents had been regular attendees at home, and occasional away games, we lived abroad from when I was four to when I was seven. The first time I was old enough to go was therefore on our return to England in 1971, although I cannot remember attending a match that season, even with the aid of looking at the fixtures for that campaign.

There was, however, one guaranteed way of checking: my mother's diaries. For those of you unfamiliar with these literary tomes, they consist of a complete record of my childhood, noting not just what happened on a particular day in time, but also notable anniversaries – not just birthdays, but events such as 'Peter nose bleed' (1968), 'Peter started school' (1969), etc. Surely there I would find the answer to the question of 'my first match'.

I was right – to a point. The 1971 diary records that on Saturday 14 August I went to football with Dad. Eagerly, I double-checked *Rothmans* to find out which game I saw, only to discover that Swindon were away at Blackpool on that day. Now I would love to be able to paint a picture of father and son going up the M5 and M6 for a day out, but sadly it wouldn't be accurate. The reason why I cannot remember my first game at the County Ground is simple. It was a reserve-team match.

Sadly (or fortunately, depending on your point of view), the 1972 diary is no more. I therefore cannot say if I saw a home first-team match in 1971/72. I can remember my parents going to watch the 1-1 home draw with Birmingham in October 1971, but this was during term-time, and an evening kick-off, and, given that I wasn't attending home Saturday 3 p.m. kick-offs, I was never going to be allowed to go. I therefore think that the first time I saw Don play live was the opening day of the 1972/73 season (Dad somehow resisted the temptation to take me to watch the reserves, probably because they weren't playing) when Swindon drew 2-2 with QPR at the County Ground, with QPR equalising near the end – what does it say about me that this goal is all I can remember of the game?

Yet Don had been my hero before then, from the first time I saw him on television. Some background is again necessary here. In the 'old days', ITV used to broadcast regional football programmes on a Sunday afternoon – you got extended highlights of the local game, and then the goals from some of the games outside your area. As each programme only had one main game, you used to spend Sunday hoping you would get a thrilling 3-3 rather than a 0-0. Living in the football metropolis that was Gloucestershire, we didn't get our own programme (there wasn't much demand for Cheltenham *v.* Enderby Town in front of 300). Instead, we were treated to the delights of *Star Soccer*, with the delightful commentary of Hugh Johns bringing you highlights of your local game, such as Stoke City *v*. Everton, or Derby County *v*. Ipswich… you get the picture. As an aside, what was even worse was Johns' commentary, which rarely bore any resemblance to the game he (and we) were watching. As a commentary technique for radio it works (I practice it most weeks), but when the audience can actually see the pictures…

Anyway, every now and then the HTV West region would do their own programme. This usually consisted of highlights of Bristol City, or if they weren't playing Bristol City reserves, or Bristol City under-fives. In an absolute emergency they would show Swindon. We couldn't get this in Cheltenham, but, for some reason that has never been satisfactorily explained to me, my paternal grandparents, living in Bishops Cleeve (five miles north of our home), could. So it was that I had my first ever glimpse of Don, as HTV West screened highlights of the Town's 4-0 victory over Fulham. Don scored twice, and I was hooked.

Fast-forward over thirty years. Here is the story of Swindon's greatest ever footballer. In cricket, aficionados of the summer game know that 'The Don' can only ever refer to Don Bradman. In Wiltshire, and to a degree in SE25, London, say the word 'Don', and everyone knows you're talking about Donald Edward Rogers, The Swindon Flyer.

A Somerset Boy

It may come as a surprise to many that Wiltshire's favourite football son was actually born in the neighbouring county of Somerset. It may come as even more of a surprise to know that he was born in a mining village: the West Country has many different attractions, but mining would not generally be seen as one of them.

Donald Edward Rogers was born on 25 October 1945, the middle of the three children raised by Ernest (known to everyone as Jim) and Agnes Mary (known as Mary). He has an older sister, Brenda, and a younger brother, Robert. The three children arrived within three years, which made life a little hectic (and presumably noisy) in the Rogers household. Home for Don was the village of Old Mills, near Paulton (which is the place generally given as Don's birthplace in the record books), but his birthplace was most definitely a village with just forty houses – more of a hamlet in fact.

Around 200 yards from Don's house was a mine and it was there that Don's father worked. Don recalls that his father was adamant that his son would 'never go down the mine' – indeed, he felt so strongly about this that Don was never allowed to go and visit his father's workplace, even on 'open days'. It was a hard life: Jim got up every day at 4.30 a.m. and worked his shift from 6 a.m. to 2 p.m.

Unsurprisingly, when Don came home from school he recalls that his father would usually be having a quick nap.

It was a happy home, even if the combination of the low wages of a miner and the demands of three children meant that there wasn't much money to go round. Not that this bothered the young Don. Living in the country he was far too busy doing 'all the things you wouldn't do today', such as picking apples from the local orchard (scrumping to the uninitiated), or 'jumping rivers'. Yet from an early age, football featured highly in Don's life: 'I was lucky in that there were twelve or fourteen lads all born within three years in the village, which meant we could always make up two teams. Looking back on it, it was amazing where we played – there were sticks and stones all over the pitch. Sometimes the dads would join in and then it would be lads versus dads, and about twenty of us would be playing.'

Don's father played local league football for Clapton All-Stars; he was a centre forward – Don recalls, with a laugh that he was a 'good header of the ball, which is quite funny' (great footballer that he was, few would ever associate Don with much aerial ability). However, one thing that Don did inherit from his dad was speed...

We used to live at house number five, and my dad's father used to live at number sixteen. Every night my dad used to go to my grandad's to play crib, and I used to go along to watch. At the end of the evening we used to race back from number sixteen to number five – about 100 yards. Dad would set off and I would try and catch him. I was thirteen or fourteen before I could beat him because he was very quick. Once I started to beat him, he stopped!

Crib featured highly in Don's childhood, even now if he challenges you to a game, think twice about it... 'I can play crib very well, which comes from playing with my grandfather. In the summer I used to play with him ten hours a day, and then again in the evening with my dad. I'm exceptionally good at adding up in my head even now, and that comes from playing so much crib. I know people say playing cards is bad for you, but there can be some good points!'

Back to the football, and by the age of thirteen, Don was playing in his first organised league games. His team were the local youth club, Thickett Mead. This was hard work, because, the team, being drawn from the village, didn't have enough players of the required age, therefore Don was playing against seventeen-year-olds. It was a new experience for him: 'I remember playing against a guy called Derek Baber, who was the right-back for the best team. He was twice as big as me and used to frighten me to death! It was the first time I can remember playing against people who were much older and bigger.'

Unsurprisingly, Thickett Mead struggled, but the young Don would extend his footballing experience, firstly by playing in the school team, and then by representing Somerset Schoolboys. At school, he played centre half. He was the best player, and the tactics were very simple – give the ball to Don, and he would run from one half to the other. He also ended up as Head Boy at the school, Paulton Secondary Modern. Don is convinced that it must have been because of his sporting prowess, as he 'never said boo to a goose'.

Representative honours followed with Somerset Schoolboys, whom he captained twice at football, and as an accomplished athlete he also competed strongly in district sports, although he recalls being beaten into second place each year in the sprint events by the same person as he moved up the age groups.

By the age of fourteen, Don was attracting the interest of League clubs. In 1959, the year before Don left school, Bert Head, the manager of Swindon Town, had 'taken his name and address' having seen him play, but by the autumn of 1960, with Don planning to leave school at Christmas the race for the quiet, slight winger was hotting up. Don cannot remember now all the scouts who came to watch, but what he can recall is how close he came to signing for Swindon's bitter rivals, Bristol City:

Fred Ford, then at Bristol City, was very keen, but he just missed out. Bert Head came and picked my dad up, drove him to a game at Swindon, drove him back, and I signed there and then. An hour and a half later, Fred Ford turned up at my house to sign me, but it was too late.

It would be good to record that the young Don and his dad had talked at length about which club he should join, and had concluded that Swindon, with Head developing a side based on youth, would be the best bet. The truth is somewhat different; Don is honest enough to admit that neither he or his dad made any allowance for this – they just signed!

So in January 1961, the young Don, still only fifteen, left home for the first time and headed for Swindon. Bert Head picked him up personally, and took him to the club's hostel in Shrivenham Road, run by Mr and Mrs Pigeon – 'lovely people' as Don remembers, although it didn't stop him from being 'absolutely petrified' and 'very pleased to get home at the weekends'.

Don soon settled into the daily routine of being on the ground staff – cleaning the boots, sweeping the stands, and doing 'any other odd jobs that were needed'. At weekends though, it was football, playing for the A team...

We used to play in the Wiltshire Premier League one week and the Hellenic League the other week. You used to get kicked all over the park playing in the Wiltshire League, but at least you could play in the Hellenic League. The sides such as Radstock, Peasdown and Paulton though, were all keen to kick me, because I'd left Somerset to come to Swindon, and they didn't like that.

Keith Morgan, who would later be Don's captain in the first team, recalls somebody who you could soon see was a talented player: 'Don was a very quiet and unassuming young boy when he joined us, but you could soon see that he was a cut above the normal players. I used to go and watch him play before he was in the first team, and his ability was incredible for such a young player. You knew he was going to make it.'

Paul Plowman, in his invaluable book *Swindon Town: To Wembley and Beyond*, notes that Don's debut for the club came against Pressed Steel in a Hellenic League game in mid-January 1961. His first goal for the club came against Hungerford (a team he would later manage) on 25 March 1961. Don (who has a variable memory of games and goals), could remember nothing about this, although he did recall playing against the Berkshire side. What is clear though, is that the young Rogers progressed well in his first calendar year at the club, to the point where, by 1962, aged just sixteen, he was playing for the reserves: 'I know I played for the reserves in early 1962, although I can't remember any of the games. What I do know though, is that after one of the games, the *Adver* (the local Swindon evening paper, or *Evening Advertiser*, to give it its full title) had a go at me. Somewhere it's written down in print that I'd never be good enough…'

Don also played in the FA Youth Cup of 1961/62, a competition in which he was later to make a real name for himself. His early outing though wasn't quite so memorable, as Swindon lost at home 3-2 to non-League Weymouth: 'It wasn't taken very well by Bert Head, and so he sacked half the people who didn't play, on the grounds that if they couldn't get into a side that was beaten by Weymouth, they couldn't be very good. It always struck me as a bit unfair, but I suppose he had a point.'

Weymouth features strongly in the Rogers story in those early days at Swindon, for it was on the pre-season tour to Weymouth in the summer of 1962 that Don had his first prolonged exposure to the first team:

We went down to Weymouth for pre-season training for two weeks, and had a great time – it was brilliant. We were on 'jankers', so we had to do things like get the breakfasts and prepare all the vegetables, as well as train. We were all in one big tent, players and management, so you imagine what that was like, especially after a few beers! Curfew was 10.30 p.m. and nobody was late, but all the cars would come in at 10.25 p.m. – never quarter-past or earlier!

The football was good too. Don recalls a game against the unusual opposition of Portland Prison, and then playing, and scoring, against the local side, Weymouth.

I remember scoring against Weymouth down there – I ran across the goal, and as I went to hit it, it bobbled and looped over the goalkeeper's head: the luckiest goal in the world really, but the local press said what a great goal it was. Funnily enough, I did the same thing at Reading a few years later and again everybody said what a great goal. It's funny, isn't it, that when you get a name for doing something good it sticks and you get away with things?

Don, as his wont, is being modest. Fluke or no fluke at Weymouth, his performances were causing those in the club to take notice. Even though he was only sixteen his talent was very evident, and he was knocking on the door of first-team football.

In the First Team

In order to fully understand the Don Rogers story, it is important to understand something about the town in which he was to make his name, and to know more about the club with which he will always be associated.

Although in recent years, Swindon has become known as one of Europe's fastest-growing towns, on the back of companies such as Honda, WH Smiths, Hambro Life (later Allied Dunbar and Zurich Life), Nationwide and Motorola to name but a few, establishing operations in the town, for much of the nineteenth and twentieth centuries the town meant one thing – railways. The link with railways started in 1843 when Great Western established a repair and maintenance facility in what was then a greenfield site near the junction of the Great Western main line; this facility was quickly expanded to include the building of locomotives in 1846 and the establishment of the Carriage and Wagon Works in 1868. By 1900 the 'old' community of the small market town of Swindon, and the 'new' community of the works, had joined together to form the Borough of Swindon.

Tim Bryan, of the Great Western Railway Museum at Swindon, writing in Richard Tomkins and Peter Sheldon's book, *Swindon and the GWR*, records that 'by the outbreak of the First World War,

Swindon Works had become the heart of the Great Western system, producing almost everything needed to run its operation' and later 'in the years before the Second World War, the life of the whole town was dominated by the company's operations'.

The railway works were the town's major employer by some distance; indeed, one of my own early childhood memories is hearing the hooter that would sound for the start of the working day across the town. The town's population then was much less itinerant than it is today, therefore the sense of community and depth of relationship with the area was stronger. That relationship included the link between many of the railwaymen and the football club. The hours of the works were 6.00 a.m. to 5.30 p.m. (with breaks), Monday to Friday, and then 6.00 a.m. to midday on Saturday, at which point many people clocked off and went to watch their football team…

The local football team were known by a variety of names: The Railwaymen, The Robins (until the ridiculous decision to change the clubs badge in the 1980s, the club crest had both a Robin and a steam engine on it), or, if you lived in the area, simply 'The Town'. They were formed in 1881, by the Reverend William Pitt, in order, as Dick Mattick records in his history of the club, 'to provide recreation for the young men of his parish'. After playing in various local leagues, they entered the Southern League, as founder members in 1894 (in the days when there were only two divisions and thirty-two clubs within the Football League).

Early on, progress in the Southern League was limited, but this changed with the arrival of Swindon's most famous player before Don – Harold Fleming. Fleming played for Swindon from 1907 to 1924, and had a huge impact on the side's fortunes. Not only that, but he was also capped 9 times at full international level by England – making him the only player ever to have that distinction while playing for the club. With Fleming a key member of the team, not only did Southern League fortunes improve to the point where the side were runners-up in successive seasons, 1908/9 and 1909/10, but he also inspired two great FA Cup runs, both of which resulted in appearances in the semi-finals. Sadly, both ties were lost – to Newcastle in 1910, and then to Barnsley in 1912, after a replay, where Swindon were without Fleming who was injured (or deliberately maimed, depending on which account you choose to believe) during the first game. Some compensation was to be found in a first ever Southern League Championship in 1914 after a season in which The Railwaymen knocked Manchester United out of the FA Cup.

In 1921 the Football League decided to admit all the clubs of the Southern League into the fold, thereby creating a Third Division. Swindon were founder members, and they were to stay in this division under a further League reorganisation in 1958 which brought together the Third Division (South) and Third Division (North) to form the Third and Fourth Divisions. In order to gain promotion from the Third Division (South) to the Second Division, a club needed to win the division – no play-offs in those days. The best Swindon could manage was fourth place, on four occasions: 1920/21 (their first season in the League), 1946/47 (when centre forward Harry Morris scored 47 League goals), 1948/49, and then, most importantly, in 1957/58 – a position which gave them a place in the newly formed Third Division.

That fourth place in 1957/58 was in fact a remarkable achievement. Between 1949 and 1957, Swindon had become what Mattick describes as 'one of the disaster areas of League football'. Financially, the club had struggled, despite regular gates of 8,000, and on the field the club had finished in the bottom half of the table every season from 1949/50 through to 1956/57, the nadir being reached in 1955/56 when they finished bottom of the entire League.

The performance in 1956/57 was scarcely better, with a rise of just one place to twenty-third, but in retrospect this was the season in which the club's fortunes began to improve. On 3 October 1956, the board decided to appoint the team's first ever manager (previously, as at many clubs, the side had been selected by committee). The man they chose was the assistant manager at Bury. His name was Bert Head.

John Trollope holds the League record for the most appearances for one club: one that in this day and age of agents, Bosman transfers and general insecurity in the football world will surely never be broken. As one who played at the County Ground for twenty years, he is a great source of information and anecdotes on a big chunk of Swindon's post-war history. He remembers the man who gave him, and Don, his debut: 'We've got a lot to thank Bert Head for – and we were lucky that he was looking to change things after we'd gone through a bad patch as a club – some of the football I saw as a young lad in the 1950s wasn't very good! Mind you, I'm not sure he'd get away with some of the things he used to say to us in today's climate!'

In the dizzy heights of the Third Division, Swindon struggled to make much of an impact, finishing fifteenth and sixteenth in their first couple of seasons. However, behind the scenes things were changing. Head realised that, with the state of the club's finances still parlous, the only way forward was to develop young talent. He soon found himself with the beginnings of the team that were to become known as 'Bert's Babes'. The traditional pre-season trial match between 'The Probables' (the first team) and 'The Possibles' (the reserves) for the 1960/61 season was won by the Possibles 7-2, and they won again when Head replayed the game behind closed doors. As a result, Head decided to go with youth, and players such as John Trollope, Terry Wollen and Cliff Jackson were given their debuts, to join other youngsters such as Bobby Woodruff, Ernie Hunt and Mike Summerbee, who had already been given their chance in their first team.

Although Head's young side finished sixteenth in 1960/61, the foundations were being laid, and with Ernie Hunt scoring 18 goals the following season, the club were up to ninth. The scene was set for a memorable 1962/63 season… and the debut of a winger from Somerset. John Trollope could see what Head was trying to do: 'There were a load of us who all came into the team at that time – all under twenty – Mike Summerbee, Ernie Hunt, Keith Morgan, Terry Wollen, Bobby Woodruff and me. He knew things had to change, so he gave us all a chance and it came off.'

The team was now starting to become established. Mike Turner was the goalkeeper, who had become the regular custodian towards the end of the previous season, taking over from the long-serving Sam Burton. The full-backs were both products of the youth scheme, Terry Wollen and John Trollope, as was Bobby Woodruff at wing back. The other half-backs were longer-serving players: Keith Morgan, who had made his debut in 1958, and the highly experienced centre half and club captain Maurice Owen, a Town regular since just after the Second World War.

The right side of attack featured two players who would go on and have successful First Division careers, Mike Summerbee at outside right and Ernie Hunt at inside right. Hunt would once again be top scorer at the end of the season, with 24 League goals. The left side was a little less settled, the duties being shared primarily between local player Roger Smart, who had made his debut the previous season, former England schoolboy international Cliff Jackson, and Arnold Darcy, Bert Head's first signing back in 1956. Jack Smith was a regular scorer at centre forward. It was an exciting and developing team as John Trollope recalls: 'We could see that if Bert could keep us together we'd have success, although even then you knew that some of the players would go on and play at a higher grade.' Keith Morgan agrees:

> We knew we had a good team, and were as good as anybody. I don't think we really discussed promotion, because you don't want to tempt fate, but we were aware that we were part of something that was developing.

Two of the first four games were lost, but then only three of the next fifteen games, including one at Halifax, where despite leading 3-0 with thirteen minutes to go, Swindon managed to lose 4-3. No matter, they soon bounced back, and a 1-1 draw with Reading took them to within two points of the top of the table. As Mattick records, everyone was doing well at this stage. Bert Head was rewarded with a pay increase and a five-year contract and the players were on a bonus for every thousand (spectators) over 9,500, home and away. Those players would have enjoyed seeing a crowd of nearly 22,000 at Ashton Gate for the 2-2 draw at Bristol City, and the 16,000 gate for the home draw with Reading.

By the middle of November, after a 4-3 win at Millwall, the side were clearly going to be challenging for promotion. The next game, on 17 November, was at home to Southend United. It was time for the entry of a new addition to Bert's Babes – Don, who had just turned seventeen. The man who played behind him at left-back, John Trollope, was not surprised at the youngster's promotion: 'I knew Don, obviously, because the professionals and the ground staff used to change in the same dressing room. He was a very quiet lad, but his talent was obvious even then – you could see he had more ability than most of us that had broken through.' Don's debut finally came because of somebody else's misfortune, as the man himself explains:

> I was hoping that I might get a game towards the end of the season, and I think that might have been what Bert Head had in mind. However, Arnold Darcy got injured and I was in. I was very, very nervous, but once I got on the pitch I was fine. I don't remember any details about the game at all though.

Today, one might expect promising youngsters to have their first taste of league football from the substitutes bench, but in those days there wasn't one substitute allowed, let alone five. Don was brought in and expected to play for the whole game. To settle his nerves, Jack Smith scored twice in the first ten minutes as Swindon won 4-1 in front of 10,296. Keith Morgan was Don's skipper that day:

> There was no surprise when Don got picked, because everyone could see he was ready. I remember going round and seeing him in the dressing room to wish him all the best, to try and settle him down – he was nervous, but then everybody is on their debut, whether they show it or not.

The young winger kept his place for the next six League and cup games, scoring his first goal for the team in the 3-1 home win over Notts County on 1 December, although that game was marred by a serious injury to Terry Wollen that would ultimately force him to retire. This game is the first one Don can recall:

> The first game I can really remember was the game against Notts County when Terry broke his leg – a real tragedy that was – both for him and for the club. I know I scored but I don't know how it went in! I tell you though, I wouldn't have celebrated how they do today – jumping into the crowd and everything. They know they're going to get booked, so why do they do it? We just put our arms in the air and trotted back to the halfway line! I also remember going down to Yeovil in the cup (in fact this was Don's second game). The slope there was massive – it really was, and they really fancied their chances against us, but we won and winning your first games in any team helps you settle in – everyone is happier as a result – especially the manager!

He scored again in the 5-0 home win over Queens Park Rangers on 12 January 1963, when, owing to the poor weather, Swindon played in Bata Basketball boots, with rubber soles. This is one game Don is unlikely to forget:

> Nobody could stand up – we were slipping and sliding about even though we had the basketball boots on. They were playing in moulded studs and they didn't stand a chance. Nowadays the match would never have taken place – in fact the referee wouldn't bother even having a look... The basketball boots were Bert Head's idea. We used to train in them, so we were used to them. Harry Cousins was the trainer then, and he was so miserly that if you got a hole in one of your boots, you didn't get a new pair, you just got a new right boot, or left boot. We were all playing in odd boots!

Unsurprisingly, Swindon's continued good form attracted many admirers. Bert Head was approached to manage Peterborough United, then in the same division, but turned the offer down, much to Don's relief:

> Bert was great for us to play for because he really did believe in giving youth a chance. A proper chance too – there's no point in giving someone just one or two games, you need to give them a decent run. Looking back, if you talk to any of us who played with him – Trolly (John Trollope), Mick Summerbee, Ernie Hunt – we'd all say the same: we were really fortunate to have had him as our first manager. Don't overlook Harry Cousins either – he did a great job too, although he was as hard as nails; he used to join us in training and kick us all about – you learned quickly how to get out of the way, or you got hurt. The story about Harry that we all knew was one from his playing days – not a nice story really, but it tells you what it was like back then – Harry was told to 'look after' their number eight by the manager. Anyway, after five minutes this number eight is injured after a tackle by Harry, who said he didn't need to look because he could 'hear the blood'!

While the League form had been excellent, an FA Cup run was also developing. Don had played in rounds two and three, away victories at Yeovil and Luton respectively. This set up Don's first 'big' match, a home cup tie against First Division Everton at the County Ground. A crowd of over 26,000, Swindon's highest attendance for many years, turned up to see if they could pull off an upset. It was not to be. Everton were four up at half-time, and eventually won 5-1. For Don it was an education:

> They were a brilliant side, absolutely brilliant – one of the best sides I ever played against in my career. They murdered us, and all we could do was really watch and admire it. I know I didn't get a kick. The funny story about that game is that I was working on the pitch in the morning, as one of the young pros – I didn't do that

much, but there was no question of anyone letting me off my duties, even though I would be playing later. We all had to help – putting sand on the pitch mainly – the game would never have been on otherwise.

Somehow it is difficult to see Wayne Rooney being asked to do the same thing before an important cup tie in 2004. For Don, that was the end of first-team action for the season, other than one appearance at home to Bournemouth (or Bournemouth & Boscombe Athletic as they were called then) in the promotion run-in. The seventeen-year-old had been used sparingly, and he ended the season with 10 League and cup appearances: 'I basically played when Arnold was out injured. Once he was fit again, I dropped out. I had no problem with that – he was the first choice, and we all knew that.'

John Trollope, looking back at that season as a former manager of the club himself, approves of Bert Head's treatment of his young star: 'Bert blooded him very carefully. Don was a quiet person, and was still very young, and I think Bert was a bit concerned about Don's confidence if things hadn't gone right.'

Don was a frustrated observer for the last five games of the season as his team sought to secure promotion to the Second Division. While he would have much preferred to have been playing, he was at least able to celebrate, along with the rest of the team, when Roger Smart's late winner against Shrewsbury on 14 May sealed their elevation in status. After over forty years of League football, Swindon Town had their first promotion, one which Don is sure the side deserved:

We were a very good side to watch, especially at home. We had a great home record that season didn't we? (18 wins out of 23 games with 60 goals scored in those games). At home we never felt we were going to lose. There were also players in that team who were obviously playing at a level lower than they should have been – people like Ernie, Mike and Bobby, but also some of the lads who stayed at Swindon, like Roger Smart and John Trollope.

The summer saw what could have been a hugely significant event: the signing of England youth international Graham French from Luton Town. French was signed to be the first choice in Don's preferred position of left wing. It seemed that while Bert Head was a great admirer of Don's talent, he wasn't yet convinced that his prodigy (still only seventeen) was ready for the weekly demands of Second Division football. Don can still recall the signing:

> Graham French was a brilliant player, absolutely superb. He was the best player I ever saw at selling a dummy – preparing to cross the ball, and then not crossing it. He would have been first choice, but he got a groin injury in pre-season and was out for a long time, and then by the time he was fit, I was established. I was just lucky really; I've always said that luck plays a major part in your career.

Keith Morgan agrees that French was a great player, but does not think he was better than Don:

> Graham French was a big star back then – a bit of a prodigy because he'd played for England schoolboys and scored a couple of goals at Wembley. He was a very good player, but I don't think he was as skilful as Don.

The start by the team in the Second Division was nothing short of sensational. The first six matches were all won to take Swindon to the top of the table, the last of the matches – a home win against just-relegated Manchester City – being won 3-0, to make the country sit up and take notice. John Trollope recalls the game against City as 'one that a lot of the older supporters will remember as the best ever game at the County Ground'. For his part, Don, while agreeing that the Manchester City game was 'something a bit special', thinks that the game at Portsmouth, which Swindon won 4–1 was 'even better, particularly as it was away from home. It made a lot of people sit up and take notice.'

None of the first nine games were lost, and this time Don featured in a cup giant-killing when First Division Chelsea were beaten 3–0 in the League Cup, a new competition then in its third season. The first defeat didn't come until the tenth match, a 4–0 capitulation at Northampton, and Swindon were still in the top four at the end of October, after a 4–2 away victory over Plymouth where Don scored for the second successive match. Funnily enough that game against Northampton has stuck in Don's memory, despite the heavy defeat:

> Northampton away: what a game that was. Frank Large (who later that season would sign for Swindon), was, how shall we say, an old-fashioned centre forward, and he volleyed Ken McPherson's boot over the stand – after the boot had come off Ken's foot, I hasten to add! They were a frightening side Northampton, a big ugly back five (at which point Don rattles their names off at great speed, so they obviously made an impact) – you didn't get in the way of them.

Don is quick to point out that there were a number of reasons for the good start:

> Firstly, and foremost, we were a really good side, as shown by the number of players who went on to play at a higher level. We were a young side too, and that helped, because it meant that we went out and just played – we didn't have any fear, we took every game on its merits and our confidence grew as we were more successful.

Now, a slight diversion. Late last year my wife received a telephone call from my father-in-law to say that there was a programme on digital television (BBC Three to be precise) about Swindon Town.

I have to say that initially I was sceptical – Swindon Town Football Club do not feature in many television programmes, even on obscure digital channels. Yet to his credit, my father-in-law was right, and the programme was a gem. Entitled *Seven Days to Saturday*, it followed a week in the life of Swindon Town in October 1963.

The programme, in good, old-fashioned, black and white, begins with the team en route back from their match at Preston, where they had lost 1-0: a long journey back in those (mainly) pre-motorway days. The film then follows the team over the week. We see them training on the County Ground pitch, and then away from the club. Don, called Donald throughout the thirty-minute duration of the documentary, is seen entering a sweet shop, playing football in the street, and getting in his car to visit his mother. The *pièce de résistance* was some real action, taken from the home game with Leyton Orient on 19 October 1963. The programme makers must have been overjoyed – what a game to choose. Swindon won 5-0 with Don scoring one of the goals, and he was delighted when the programme was shown again:

> I don't remember the programme being made, but I saw it when it was shown recently and it was great. Mind you, I think some of the stuff was done for the benefit of the cameras – for example, I was shown going to visit my mum with my club blazer on – I thought, 'Oh yeah, I would have worn that wouldn't I?' The other thing that struck me was the number of people going to the match with ties on –presumably people going straight from work. The programme also called me Donald, which I don't like, only two or three people ever call me that – Clive King, the old *Adver* reporter used to be one. I didn't like that!

Keith Morgan would beg to differ about Don's dress sense: 'Don was always incredibly smart in his blazer and tie – we used to give him a lot of stick for it – he was much better dressed than any of us!'

Watching action from the game forty years later, one is struck by the apparent space afforded to the players, and the way in which Swindon's young team passed the ball around. The goals were celebrated with a simple handshake by the players, and with applause by the spectators, many of whom still wore cloth caps, and, as Don pointed out, ties. This was, indeed another era. Sadly for Don and his teammates, that win, and the win over Plymouth the following week, were to represent the high point of the season. None of the next seven games were won, and there was a run of five matches without a goal. Don has an explanation:

> just changed round completely, but that's what youngsters are likely to do – have a run of bad form, and not to be particularly consistent – and remember we were all young together as well, so once we had a few bad results we lost confidence and found it difficult to get back to winning again.

A 2-0 win at home to Portsmouth just before Christmas seemed to have stopped the rot, but this too was to give false hope. None of the next nine matches were won, as the team slipped down the table, and the defeats included a 6-0 reversal at Sunderland, who would be promoted at the end of the season. Don, who was still only eighteen, was an ever-present until the 4-1 defeat at Newcastle at the end of February, a game he missed through injury. It had been a great run, as Don recalls:

> I was so lucky really, because, as I said earlier, without Graham French getting injured I probably wouldn't have played. Once I did play and do well though, there was no way that Bert was going to drop me, not with me being a local lad, and one of his youngsters. He probably saw me as another feather in his cap – another youngster made good. From my point of view, everything just flew by, what with the Youth Cup run and England Youth.

John Trollope recalls that was the season that Don really broke through:

> I remember Don was now a real first-team regular, and we were able to develop a great understanding down the left that really helped the team. I think it was good for me that Don came in when I was established, because I had been used to playing more with Arnold Darcy who was a good honest 'up and downer' and used to give me a lot of help. Don played in the opponents' half, so I didn't always get the same help, but by then I was more experienced so it worked well.

Every now and then, however, Don would incur Keith Morgan's ire, as his former skipper admits: 'I used to really complain at him for not getting back, but he used to ignore me – he would just whistle at me! In the end we just left him up, and the opposition had to put two men on him… he'd still go past them mind!'

In the midst of the decline in League form, some solace was to be found in the FA Cup, where another good run took the team through to the fifth round. There they were drawn at home to First Division West Ham, the eventual winners of the competition. The Hammers had already ended the hopes of Swindon in the League Cup, winning 4-1 at Upton Park after a 3-3 draw at the County Ground, and they were too strong again in the FA Cup, winning 3-1 in front of a record attendance of 28,000. For Don, these experiences of playing against First Division defences were all part of his football education:

> I can only just remember those games really – I remember the matches against them later on much better. What I do recall is the crowd at Swindon: the biggest I'd seen at that stage in my career.

As the League form declined, so the first of Bert's Babes sought his fortune elsewhere. On 6 March, Bobby Woodruff was sold to Wolves for £35,000. The club did not want him to leave, and there were no pressing financial reasons for the sale, but the player was adamant that he wanted to go. Wolves would later sign Ernie Hunt, and also tried to sign Don, but that's jumping ahead in the story...

The season petered out to its close. After playing in all of the first thirty-eight League and cup games, Don played in just five of the last eleven, as the team finished fourteenth, mainly because of an extended absence with England youth, which we will hear about later. Indeed, Swindon's form when Don was away was poor (four successive defeats), and Bert Head was moved to blame the results on the absence of his winger, who had quickly become a key member of the side. Don finished with 11 League and cup goals from his 43 League and cup appearances, making him the second-top scorer behind the irrepressible Ernie Hunt. It had been some first full season:

> From my point of view, the season couldn't have gone any better really. I established myself in the first team, much sooner than I had expected, and had a great season of youth football, both for Swindon and England. The only disappointment was that we couldn't finish higher in the League, but bear in mind that it was a very young team, and it was the first time we'd all played at that level.

His long-standing friend, John Trollope, has similar thoughts: 'It was a great shame that we couldn't maintain the start really; perhaps we were just a bit too young and inexperienced. It was a great team, and had some really talented players – you knew they were going to make it in the game.'

For Don personally it had been an incredible season. Not only was he a first-team regular, but had been playing regularly for both the youth team and also for England youth:

> It was unbelievable really, because I was doing something every week: I was away with England six or seven times that year from Monday until Wednesday, quite apart from the five games I missed

because of the tournament in Holland. I must have played over sixty games, so it's not surprising that looking back things seem like a bit of a blur!

Nowadays, sixty games plus would of course be considered far too many for any professional footballer. Squad rotation and protection of young talent would see a modern-day Don used much more sparingly. Back then though, he wasn't bothered:

All I wanted to do was to play. I was young and fit, and everything was going pretty well, so I was just caught up in the buzz and excitement of it all really.

Don, at the age of eighteen, was now a first-team regular. His name was starting to be known nationally. He had arrived.

The First Great Cup Run

In his time at Swindon, Don would play a key role in getting his side through to two major national cup finals. The 1969 League Cup run is well known, but less well remembered, although arguably as great an achievement, was the Rogers-inspired run of the Wiltshire side in the FA Youth Cup of 1963/64. For that reason, it warrants a chapter in its own right.

Before we examine that cup run though, one of Don's memories from youth team days has echoes of a game when he was a first-team regular: it was a match against an Italian team that was abandoned…

> We played in a youth tournament in Belgium and got drawn to play the Italian team, Torino. The referee made a decision that angered the Italians, and they tried to persuade him to change his mind. Of course, quite rightly, he wouldn't, whereupon they lost their tempers and chased him off the field! The game was abandoned, and we were declared the winners!

Bruce Walker, who played with Don in the youth cup run, and will be best remembered for a dramatic, late, equaliser against Nottingham Forest in an FA Cup tie, recalls that Don's status as the star player was never in doubt:

I'm not ashamed to say that I tried to model myself on him. He was a year older than me, and I saw him as someone to learn from. The coaches said that the reason why he had such great balance, and this ability to swerve and beat his man, was down to the fact that he ran with one shoulder lower than the other. I tried to mimic that, but it didn't work for me – I couldn't keep my balance at all.

Walker was a winger, like Don, and he remembers one funny incident from their youth football days:

I was told this story by David Houston and Dai Yorath, who played with me at Margate. Anyway, they both played against Don and I for Cardiff youth team when we were playing for Swindon. For fifteen minutes they kicked me black and blue on the wing, and their bench were shouting encouragement at them as they did so. Then Don got the ball, went past four or five players and scored a great goal. At that point the Cardiff manager got his message out to David and Dai: they'd been kicking the wrong bloke – they'd be told to kick Don!

Don was, as we have seen, a first-team regular in 1963/64. Yet he was only seventeen in August 1963, and was thus eligible for youth-team duty. There was never any option of him giving the youth cup a miss:

There is no way that I would have been allowed to have not played. Bert always liked to play his strongest side, and I seem to recall that he tried to arrange matches so I could play.

Bert Head was always someone who would give youth a chance, and would put a high priority on the youth team, so it was perhaps unsurprising that Swindon were becoming known for the strength of talent coming through the ranks. Yet, given the strength of the youth schemes at some of the First Division teams, there was a tendency for the youth cup to follow the pattern its big brother, the FA Cup – isolated shock results, but with the finalists usually drawn from First Division clubs. Major mismatches were not uncommon, particularly in the early stages: for example, in one early round of the 1963/64 competition, Manchester United beat Barrow 14-1!

Swindon's run to the final began with a 5-4 win at Portsmouth on 16 December 1963 in the second round, and the team continued a similar free-scoring vein when they won 4-2 at Brighton on 28 January 1964, in the third round. The fourth-round 4-1 win over Plymouth Argyle on 11 February, when Don scored twice, meant fourteen goals in three games.

In the quarter-finals they met a team that would be central to the Rogers story: Arsenal. The London side were beaten 2-0 at the County Ground on 10 March, in front of a crowd of 5,607. Not that Don can add much to the tale. He was genuinely surprised when I bring the tie up:

> Did we really play Arsenal? I never knew that. That must have been some game, but I can't remember anything about it at all. That was a great achievement when you consider that we were a Second Division side.

The win took the team through to a two-legged semi-final against Queens Park Rangers, then a division below Swindon at first-team level. The Robins had little trouble in getting through, winning 2-0 away and 4-1 at home. Don scored in both legs and, with the run gaining momentum, over 11,000 saw the second leg at the County Ground on 14 April:

> Now I do remember the QPR games. They had a great side with players like the Morgan twins, Ian and Roger, and Tony Hazell. We knew we would be up against it. But we had a really good side at the back that year – they didn't take any prisoners – and that stood us in good stead against Rangers.

Clive Bettison, who was later to work closely with Don at Lambourn Sports, was the same age as the youth-team players in 1964 and he went to the majority of the youth cup games: 'Don scored a great goal in the match against QPR at Swindon: a very powerful shot from distance that went straight into the top left-hand corner, past Peter Springett, who we had all heard of because his brother, Ron, was an England goalkeeper. Don was a real problem for them all game; he completely tormented Tony Hazell, who was the QPR full-back marking him.'

If the semi-final had pitted them against a smaller club, the final would rectify that. Their opponents would be Manchester United, fresh from a derby victory over Manchester City in the other semi-final. Colin Shindler has recently covered that cup tie in his book *George Best and Twenty-One Others*, and in it he recalls the common view of the time: 'All of the United players concede that Swindon were effectively a one-man team, and that Don Rogers, the England youth international, played United by himself.'

The final was billed as that of the two wingers, Don Rogers against George Best. Best, although seven months younger than Don, had made his League debut for United the previous year and was already a major star. Alongside him would be players such as Jimmy Rimmer, who would later play (albeit only briefly because of injury) in a European Cup final with Aston Villa, together with David Sadler and John Aston, both of whom would play with Best in United's European Cup triumph of 1968. It was a star-studded side. Don and his team-mates, however, were not overawed:

> I think we were just so pleased to have got to the final because nobody was expecting us to get there at all, so there was no real pressure on us. Also remember that United were not the same force then as they are now, so it wasn't quite the same as playing their youth team today.

The first leg of the final was played at the County Ground on 27 April. In front of 17,000, Don scored first for Swindon to give them a half-time lead, but Best equalised, and the game finished 1-1. We have to rely on the match report (printed overleaf) for Swindon's star is unable to recall much of the game, although Shindler says that 'Rogers ran poor Alan Duff (the Manchester United full-back) ragged'.

Don says of the game:

> I can only vaguely remember the first leg, and I couldn't tell you much about the goal. The thing I do remember was flying up to Manchester for the second leg: the club did the right thing for us. The problem was, I was deaf for six hours after we landed and couldn't hear a thing. I'm not sure what sort of plane it was, but I'm sure it had a hole in the bottom.

Clive Bettison's memory is better. He says he can still remember the goal: 'I can it now; there was a deep cross from the right across to the left wing. Don took the ball on the run, cut back in, and beat the goalkeeper. He also hit the post from a free-kick.'

Bruce Walker says the team were all a bit overwhelmed by the final:

> The final went in an absolute blur. I can remember running out at Swindon, and being amazed at just how many people were there to watch us – you've got to remember that most of us had never played in the reserve team before, let alone played in front of a crowd before. Don of course just took it in his stride, because he was used to this level of football, but for the rest of us, it was difficult.

Hicks shines in the first leg of the Youth Cup final.

TOWN HOLD THE UNITED XI
by Malcolm Harris
(*Evening Advertiser*)

Swindon T. Youths 1 Manchester U. Youths 1

Only the courageous Tony Hicks stood between Swindon Town and heavy defeat at the County Ground last night. Due to his efforts, Swindon escaped from the F.A. Youth Cup final first leg on terms with a powerful Manchester United side.

Swindon now go to Old Trafford for the second leg on Thursday, but if they are to survive the ordeal before something like 30,000 United fans, they must give their gallant goalkeeper far more support.

England youth international Donald Rogers was the only Swindon forward to find his way through United's defence, although even his performance was for once overshadowed by Hicks.

As in the first leg of the semi-final against Queens Park Rangers, Hicks made scarcely a mistake, as, time after time, he defied Manchester's finely-poised attack. His one consolation is that the man behind the visitors' major threats, Northern Ireland international George Best, may miss Thursday's game.

For Best, a frail-but-brilliant footballer, gains his second full cap against Uruguay tomorrow, and may find four games in six days too much for him. Best it was who schemed nearly every dangerous United movement, and more than once his fierce flashing shots brought fine diving saves from Hicks.

Manchester, who won the trophy during the first five years of its existence, showed glimpses of their promise from the first whistle, with Best's skilful prompting keeping Swindon's defenders at full stretch, but the early flurry ended with Aston shooting wide of an open goal.

Rogers caused a couple of moments of near panic in the Manchester goal area before Hicks began a busy evening by saving shots from Best and centre forward David Sadler.

For half an hour chances were made and missed without bias, but it was Swindon who slipped ahead after 31 minutes. Left winger Bruce Walker slung a high cross-field pass to Rogers' foot, the outside-right accelerated round Duff, swayed inside, and hammered a ground shot past Rimmer.

The last few moments of the half saw three grand saves by Hicks – first a Kinsey drive, then a Best header and finally at the feet of Sadler.

Hicks, fresh from the applause of the crowd, was back in action within seconds of the restart, but even he was helpless when a magnificent attempt by Sadler hammered against the underside of the bar.

He defied United until the 70th minute when Best scored the elusive goal. McBride pushed a pass through an opening in Swindon's defence, and Best took the ball to the advancing Hicks before flicking it to the net. The goalkeeper could do no more than help the ball on its way.

Thereafter Swindon fell back in desperate defence, with Hicks keeping well in trim for the second leg with yet more leaping saves. Fortunately for Swindon, United were guilty of inaccurate shooting at the most vital moments. Even when they really established control in the second half, their play was a little over-eager and lacked the steadiness that brings goals.

Swindon's main weakness was at inside forward where Plumb too often found his thrusts down the middle virtually unsupported.

Although the defence took tremendous punishment without cracking, far more mistakes than usual left Hicks at Manchester's mercy.

Swindon Town: Hicks; Foscolo, Ling; Grffin, Brown, Prosser; Rogers, Peapell, Plumb, Tabor, Walker.

Manchester United: Rimmer; Duff, Noble; McBride, Farrar, Fitzpatrick; Anderson, Best, Sadler, Kinsey, Aston.

Attendance 17,000   Receipts £2,401 2s 6d

Not perhaps the most glowing report of Don's career, indeed it is interesting that the report makes no mention of Don running the United full-back Alan Duff 'ragged', but worthy of inclusion in the overall context of the Don Rogers story.

For the second leg at Old Trafford, United were clear on their tactics, as Bobby Noble, who played with Don at England youth level explains in Colin Shindler's book: 'I told Alan Duff in that Youth Cup final to give Don Rogers one early on and he wouldn't want to know after that, because he was the star man down there'.

Swindon held out until just before half time, when David Sadler scored to give the home side an interval lead. He scored again just after half-time and, although Bruce Walker pulled a goal back, Sadler completed his hat-trick and John Aston's late goal meant a 4-1 defeat for the Robins on the night, and a 5-2 aggregate defeat.

Don had no complaints: 'They beat us fairly easily up there as I recall. I do remember David Sadler causing us all kinds of problems, and we ended up well beaten. We were just pleased to have got there though.'

It was another very different experience for Bruce Walker:

> The flight up there was the first time most of us had flown in an aeroplane, so that was all new. Then at Old Trafford, when we ran out, there were 25,000 people booing us – incredible! They were a class side though, George Best could have beaten us single-handedly really, and we were just in awe of some of their players looking back. I also remember after the game when we went into the lounge there were first-team players like Denis Law handing round sandwiches – it was enough to make you go weak at the knees!

It had been a remarkable achievement. Of the eleven players who played in the final, four others would play for the Town at first-team level: goalkeeper Tony Hicks, wing half Dennis Peapell, centre forward Dick Plumb and outside left Bruce Walker. None of them had long League careers, however – while they were excellent supporting players, there was no doubt that the star of the show was Don, as John Trollope recalls:

> I was too old for the youth team then, but obviously I, like every-one else at the club, took a keen interest in what was going on. At that time, for a club like Swindon to get to the youth cup final was a tremendous feat, even more so when you think that other than Don there was no one there who went on to play 200-300 League games. They just seemed to hit it off as a team – and Don was the real gem in the side that made things happen.

Forty years on, Don is at pains to pay tribute to the team:

> It was fantastic really to do what we did. I do have to emphasise as well that we were very strong at the back, because if you look at who was kept, all the defenders were let go! We worked very hard and got on well with each other and it was superb really.

Swindon Town have never before or since reached the Youth Cup final. I hope I am wrong, but in these days of the big Premiership clubs signing up most of the available young talent, I doubt they ever will again. Forty years on it seems like as great an achievement by that team as it did at the time. Don is much too modest to agree to my assertion that without him this wouldn't have happened, pointing out most forcibly that football is a team game; but on this score he and I will have to disagree – while undoubtedly others contributed hugely, this run was inspired by one man. Five years later, he would lead another great cup run as well…

Swindon Town Regular

Don spent the summer of 1964 reflecting on what had been a whirlwind first full season. Although he insists he could have kept on playing, despite his sixty-odd matches the previous season, he spent the summer resting:

> I went back home to Somerset for most of the summer and spent time there, although as I was going out with Jane then (his future wife) I would have spent time in Swindon as well.

Don was now an established first-team player, and known throughout the game as one of the most talented young players in the country. During the 1963/64 season he had become an England youth international. and had enjoyed huge success in an end-of-season international tournament at Rotterdam. The Youth Cup run had also meant more exposure nationally, and there were many clubs checking on his progress:

> Of course we were aware of the scouts coming to watch us because we had so many good players. It was different then though, because of the way things were done and the contracts we were under – it was all very gentlemanly. If somebody wanted to

buy you they had to go to the club first and ask, and if the club said no then that was the end of the matter. We never heard about any approaches, well not officially anyway!

John Trollope says that the team knew they were high profile: 'We were always aware of people watching the team, although I think we knew that the majority of the scouts were looking at people like Mike and Ernie, and especially Don, with him having had the profile of playing for England youth.'

So Don and his teammates prepared for their second season in the Second Division. Despite the poor end to the previous campaign, optimism was high within the squad: 'We had a good young team and although we'd fallen away badly the previous season the players were basically the same, but a year older, so we thought we'd do reasonably well. We just needed to keep our confidence up, because that was very important when you have such a young team – youngsters tend not to be as consistent as older pros, and you're going to get some in-and-out games, but the key is to keep confident.'

The first day of the season saw the Town at Bury. There they lost goalkeeper Norman Oakley with a cracked collarbone. There were still no substitutes allowed (although they would be introduced for the start of the following season), so it was perhaps not too surprising that with ten fit men, and an outfield player in goal, Swindon lost 6-1. Normal services seemed to be resumed when the next two home games were won, Don scoring the winner in the second of these, a 1-0 home win against Leyton Orient, but five of the next six matches were lost, including a 4-0 defeat at Swansea and a 5-0 defeat at Portsmouth within the space of five days.

Don has only limited recollections of that season, stating 'I think I've blanked most of it out', but he does recall the poor start: 'We were leaking goals everywhere, and it was very tough. It wasn't just down to the defence though, we were all finding it hard work. It was that confidence thing again: we couldn't seem to get our confidence back after we'd taken some of those hammerings.' Keith Morgan agrees: 'When you get on a losing streak, everything seems to go against you – late goals and things like that. We just couldn't get ourselves going, and it was a tough time for the club.'

A run of only two defeats in the next seven games promised an improvement, but the next five games were lost, including a 6-1 home defeat by Newcastle United. Don has vague recollections of this one: 'I can only just about remember the Newcastle game – I wouldn't have known it was 6-1, although I do remember being well beaten by them. At home too, I bet that didn't go down too well with anybody, especially Bert Head!'

Part of the problem was in the lack of a settled side. In total, twenty-five players would play for the club, and as Head tried to turn things around new players arrived, including the former Scottish international goalkeeper Frank Haffey, and the Chelsea forward Dennis Brown. Don cannot really offer much of an explanation:

> I think this season will be a small part of the book, because I don't remember much at all. Confidence would have been key, as I've said before, and I don't think we had a settled side, which often happens if you're struggling.

John Trollope, even now, forty years on, struggles to explain what happened: 'I always felt that maybe Bert was a little too faithful to the spine of the team really, given the players we had out wide. But even so, I still don't know why we struggled given the quality of players we had.'

At the turn of the year, it was evident that Swindon would be facing a battle to avoid relegation. They had just 19 points from 25 games. Part of the problem lay in their inability to draw games: they had recorded just one in the season so far. For Don personally, it had been a frustrating time. By his own high standards his scoring record had been poor, with just 3 goals, and he needed a boost.

The New Year hinted at better things to come with a couple of wins, most notably a 2-1 win at Maine Road, where the attendance was just over 8,000 – a gate which for many years was a record low for Manchester City – but only two of the following twelve games were won: 4-1 at home to Coventry, when Don scored twice, and 4-2 at home to Northampton Town after being two goals down at half-time, when Don scored again... not that he can remember them!

The most damaging defeat in that run was the 1-0 loss at home to Middlesbrough on 3 April. Football is littered with 'if only's. Here is another one: if Swindon had drawn this game, rather than losing it, they would have survived, and Middlesbrough would have gone down.

On Good Friday, 16 April, the team gave themselves renewed hope by beating Rotherham 3-2 at the County Ground. It was, however, success at a price. Ernie Hunt had chipped a bone in the win over Northampton at the end of March but had been rushed back for this crucial game. Although he scored Swindon's first goal, he aggravated his injury to the point where he was ruled out for the rest of the season. It was, as Don recalls, a crucial blow:

> I do remember Ernie's injury, because they made a special casing to help him play. He was very important to us, and Bert would have been desperate for him to play. The thing about Ernie was he was so strong on the ball – it was very difficult to get it off him, so we could play it to him and get a breather! He was a very good passer of the ball as well, and we all knew he'd play at a higher level.

The day after the Rotherham game, Swindon were at home again, this time against Preston North End. Don scored one of the goals which meant that with ten minutes to go Swindon led 2-1. Then an unlucky own goal by Owen Dawson gave Preston an ill-deserved equaliser and robbed Swindon of a crucial point.

Swindon were now two points clear of Portsmouth, who occupied the last relegation spot, but while Town lost on Easter

Monday, 1-0 at Rotherham, Portsmouth won, which meant that the teams went into the last game of the season on level points, with Swindon ahead of Portsmouth due to their superior goal average.

There was some controversy even before the kick-off on the last day of the season, Saturday 24 April. Both Portsmouth and Swindon were away, but while Swindon's game, at Southampton, would kick-off at the usual 3.00 p.m., Portsmouth's game, at Northampton, would kick-off at 7.45 p.m. Portsmouth would have the advantage of knowing Swindon's score before they kicked-off, thereby knowing exactly how they had to approach the match – they knew they simply had to get a better result than their relegation rivals. Nearly forty years on, writing these words, it seems very unfair. It wouldn't be allowed now, as Don agrees:

> It wasn't fair at all. Portsmouth had a huge advantage knowing what they had to do. Imagine if they had been playing at the same time and they were drawing they would have had to have gone for the win, and they might have left gaps at the back. Today it would never be allowed, but back then you just got on with it.

Swindon conceded early on at the Dell, going behind after two minutes, but were level just after the half hour through Dennis Brown. A point would have left Portsmouth needing a win, but Southampton scored again, less than twenty minutes from the end, to leave Pompey needing just a draw. Don again: 'Now I do remember this one – I think it's the one game that I can recall that season. We were a bit unlucky really, and probably should have got a draw.'

Portsmouth duly got their point at already promoted Northampton and, after just two seasons, Swindon's stay in the Second Division was over. Swindon found out the result in Andover, where they had stopped en route back home. John Trollope recalls the huge let-down of relegation: 'It was all very disappointing. Given the calibre of player that we had, we should definitely have stayed in the Second Division.'

It didn't take a genius to work out why the Robins had failed to survive. Just six points were taken away from the County Ground all season, a truly dreadful away record. Don needed to be reminded of this, but afterwards was philosophical: 'Six points? Are you sure? That's shocking isn't it? Well we deserved to go down with an away record like that. Mind you, when I was at Swindon we were always very good at home and poor away. I don't really know why. I think people generally just play better at home, unless they're one of the top teams.'

While the season had been a disappointing one for the club, it had been another good one for Don on the playing front. Along with John Trollope, he had been the only ever-present in the side, and his 42 League games had produced 9 goals. Still only nineteen, he was rapidly heading for a century of appearances for his club.

Relegation often brings major change at a club, as players, managers and directors review their options. The summer of 1965 was such a time for Swindon, as the club tried to come to terms with life back in the Third Division. Within the space of four months, they had a new manager, and had transferred their two most well-known players.

First to go was Bert Head, who was sacked as a result of the relegation. With the benefit of hindsight, the decision seems very harsh: Head had lifted the side from the Third Division, which had been home for over forty years, and had only narrowly failed to keep them in the Second. For Don it was a huge blow:

> I was very surprised by Bert going. I mean he'd done a lot for the club. He'd got us promoted, and he'd made the club a lot of money by developing all these young players. I think we all had a lot to thank Bert for, because he believed in us, and wasn't frightened of giving youth its chance. Without him, that Swindon side wouldn't have happened and I think he was unlucky that he was sacked.

Many of the players were hugely shocked by the sacking. It had been Head who had given a lot of them their debuts, and been a huge influence on them as footballers. John Trollope recalls: 'I was very surprised he went, to be honest. He'd got us promotion and built a good side, and I would have thought he would have been given the chance to get us back up. But the board thought differently…'

So what was Bert Head really like? Don recalls a tough man:

> I was a bit frightened of him really – I think we all were, and that got us playing a bit. We were all young and looked up to him, and did what he said. I remember contract negotiations – well, there were none really – if he said sign this, then you did. This first contract I signed, I had no idea what I was signing up for at all.

Frightened or not, Don's favourite Bert Head story is one from the 1962/63 campaign:

> That season, the winter was terrible and there was snow on the ground most of the time, so we couldn't train properly, and we used to play rugby. Bert used to join in, and when he got the ball, we all used to just jump on him – his own side as well – so there were twenty blokes on top of him in the snow!

Another time, Bert also came off the worst:

> He was driving along and he saw a group of us and stopped to give us a bollocking for something. He got out of his car to tell us off, and then got back in and drove off, but forgot to shut the car door – and smashed it against a post. We all thought it was hilarious, but couldn't show it in front of Bert.

For most of the Swindon team, it was au revoir to their former manager and their paths would not cross again. For Don, it was merely adieu; Bert Head had not finished with him yet.

The new manager was to be Danny Williams, previously manager of Rotherham United, for whom he had also played over 450 games. What did Don know of him?

> I'd never heard of him at all before he joined us, so I didn't know what to expect. I know it sounds a bit rude, but we couldn't understand what he was saying! He was really Northern in his accent, and he used different words to what we were used to. He was always cheerful though – jolly I guess you'd call it – and was a bit different to Bert in that respect.

The new man soon made an impression on his new charges:

> He always used to give us one hard day of training. We did that every week when he was here – hard running. It was usually on Thursdays and we were always talking about it on Wednesday, dreading it! It only lasted three-quarters of an hour, but you were well gone at the end of that. We used to have to put rings on and off the corner flags, and run diagonally across the pitch against someone to do it. Then we used to run round the County Ground. I was always shattered and near the back, except for the sprints. Then we used to do about fourteen laps around the County Ground, and people like Stan Harland, Roger Smart and John Trollope used to go off into the distance. My main aim was to make sure that they didn't lap me! We didn't like it, but it served us well.

Williams was appointed on 8 Jun 1965. He walked into a club in some disarray – financially, where there was a significant deficit as a result of transfer dealings, and on the playing side, where both Mike Summerbee and Ernie Hunt, two of the stars, had indicated that they wanted to leave. After some deliberation the board agreed to both requests, with Summerbee to be sold immediately and Hunt after the first two games of the season (in fact he played in the first five matches). They duly departed, Summerbee to Manchester City, and Hunt to Wolves, as Don recalls:

I hadn't realised that they left so close together, but it makes sense – they were big friends and they went round together – with Bobby Woodruff as well before he went. They were a bit older than me, of course. Mike Summerbee was a great player, really strong on the ball and a superb crosser, there was none better that I saw. He just got better and better after he left.'

In the very early part of the season, aided by seven points from their first four away matches (more, you will recall, than the received on their travels in the entire 1964/65 season), Swindon briefly topped the table, but this was ultimately a season of transition. New players included goalkeeper Peter Downsborough, fullback Joe Butler, and Welsh international centre half Mel Nurse. Danny Williams was building a side:

I think we knew that things would change under a new manager. It's always an interesting time when someone new comes in. The thing I remember though is all the new accents coming in – Peter Noble's was the worst, although I know he came later, but I couldn't understand a word he was saying. Mind you it took me a while to understand Joe Butler too (Our readers may deduce from Don's comments about the various accents that it probably never occurred to him that they may have found his Somerset burr just as difficult!) Mel Nurse was a huge man, a real colossus in defence. I remember him signing and asking who the goalkeeper was. When he found out that it was Peter, he went round the dressing room repeating to himself Peter, Peter, Peter, Peter, Peter Downsborough so he didn't forget the name. He had us in stitches!

When the side were on song, they were unstoppable. In one spell in the autumn they scored twenty goals in four successive games, but they also had a spell, towards the end of the season, where they didn't score for five games. In fact none of the last seven games were won as the side finished seventh, fourteen points behind second-place Millwall.

Don can remember little about the season:

> It was a rebuilding process really. We had a lot of new players in key
> positions and a new manager – although we did well to come
> seventh, I think. What I do recall though is that I started to score
> goals. Whether it was down to Danny Williams or not I don't
> know, but I suddenly realised that I could score, rather than just
> play left wing. For four years or so I'd just created really and stayed
> out on the wing, which was due to being brought up by Bert, who
> always said 'Left foot on the touchline' whenever we had the ball.
> Then I started, once Bert had gone, and possibly because I was that
> bit more confident – having been in the first team for a while –
> making runs inside the full-back, rather than cutting outside him. I
> probably did it once and it worked, so I decided that I could do it
> and then kept on doing it.

Not that his new manager always saw eye to eye to with his star
winger. Danny Williams caused real controversy, when, towards the
end of the season, in a speech to the Swindon Rotary Club at the
Goddard Arms, he made the following comments: 'Don sleeps
twenty minutes of a match. He's not a busy player. He's a good
player if he's got the ball – but not if he hasn't.' The *Evening
Advertiser*, reporting the speech, went on to say: 'Mr Williams added
that he could train Rogers as hard as he liked, but he could not
control him on the pitch. Despite this, he said 'we owe a lot of our
goals to Don Rogers.'

After this incident, which Don now describes as a 'storm in a
teacup', the town of Swindon, if one is to judge from the letters
page of the *Evening Advertiser*, rose to Don's defence. R.S. Payne of
Swindon wrote that 'A craftsman such as Don does not do donkey
work', while C.G. Le Poidevin of Purton wrote 'Instead of training
Rogers harder, train the other nine players to play to him' and
A.E.F. Sargent of Swindon wrote: Danny does not understand a
player of Don's calibre. Don is like Stanley Matthews. He is a

match–winner and the bulk of the 13,000 that Danny talks about are there to see him.'

Many of the letters are in a similar vein, although surely A.E. Harper of Wootton Bassett went too far when, after indicating his dissatisfaction with the team's performances during the season, he wrote that he 'would go and support Oxford United if they go up'.

Despite this, as Don says, it was his best to date in terms of goalscoring – a total of 18 in the League – and once again he was an ever-present. He also achieved one very notable landmark, his first hat-trick at first-team level, in the 6-0 home win over York City on 19 October, days before his twentieth birthday:

> It was a night game and I scored all three down at the Town End in the second half. We always wanted to play towards the Town End in the second half in those days. Mind you, one of the goals was direct from a corner, so I'm not sure it was a real hat-trick!

Keith Morgan remembers an incident after the game:

> Don played very well that night; he caused them all sorts of problems. Anyway, one of their defenders was Charlie Williams, the guy who became a comedian, and after the game he came to see me to ask where he could get some food, so I took him up to York Road to get some fish and chips before they caught the train home!

Don was adamant that this was his only hat-trick for Swindon, indeed of his career. The record books say otherwise – three other hat-tricks for his local team, all in the next three seasons. When I tell him, aided by the statistical records I take with me to help jog his memory during our meetings, he seems genuinely amazed.

Just over two weeks after the York game, Don was destroying another visitors' defence – this time Reading's. Paul Plowman's official guide to Swindon's history only credits the winger with two goals, but contemporary reports give him another hat-trick. Here is the view of an opposition reporter.

DAZZLING DONALD SINKS READING

by Roger Ware
(Reading Evening Chronicle)

Swindon (3) 5 Reading (0) 0

Reading chief Roy Bentley was not at Swindon on Saturday – he was away on Phase One of the player-hunt which has been inevitable for some weeks now. 'I nearly dropped through the floor when I heard the result' he told me – and I daresay he would have dropped through the floor, or at least would have wanted to, had he been there.

For the first time this season Reading looked out of their depth, not so much outclassed by Swindon, as by one man – Donald Rogers. I have watched Swindon many times, and from what I have seen Rogers is either downright brilliant or utterly profligate.

Unfortunately for Bentley's desperately shuffled side, this temperamental wonder boy chose Saturday 6 November to be Dazzling, Devastating, Donald. In 21 minutes at the start of the second half, Rogers turned on a display which was, without exaggeration, world-class. He was unstoppable. With three spectacular high speed runs, he crushed Reading single-handed with a superb hat-trick.

Before that, things were pretty even, with Swindon perhaps just ahead on points. Reading had created some good chances and fluffed them, Swindon's raids were halted by some neat saves by Mike Dixon.

The only score was an unsatisfactory scrambled Swindon goal in the first minute – a goal that would never have been scored had the ball not reared viciously off the pitch as Dixon went to make a simple catch. Swindon were lucky not to concede an 11th-minute equaliser when McDonald fired carelessly wide of a glaring goal, and when the reliable John Trollope got away with a blatant handball in the goalmouth after losing control of a bouncing ball. Reading were lucky when Dennis Brown, the boy from Whitley, hashed a couple of good self-created opportunities.

Then came the Rogers magic. In the 48th minute he jinked through alone from the left wing and steered the ball wide of Dixon. In a brief spell of Reading pressure Dawson cleared off the Swindon line from a Webb header, but then it was back to Donald. A few brilliant shuffles of the feet sent him through again and this time he blitzed the ball in from the edge of the penalty box, stinging Dixon's fingertips on the way. In the 70th-minute came a carbon copy, and this time Dixon did not even get a touch as the ball thundered into the corner.

The man I felt sorry for was Colin Meldrum, switched to right-back to cut out the Rogers threat. Meldrum failed in his prime mission, but to be fair, I don't think many First Division full-backs would have stopped the local hero in this form. One man I did not feel sorry for was Pat Terry. He was booked in the second half for arguing with the referee, and, though I often sympathise with Terry for the victimisation he sometimes suffers from referees, he had absolutely no excuse this time. Played out of the game by Mel Nurse, Terry carried on a continual bickering session with Mr Osborne which just had to end with his name going down in the book. Inside forwards Doug Webb and Denis Allen worked hard, but almost alone, only Terry McDonald, in occasional flashes, giving them any support.

Despite that unhappy 5-0 scoreline the defensive experiment, though far from a success, was not all that bad. Had Rogers not suddenly taken a hand I fancy Swindon might have struggled, for, apart from the outside-left, only Brown carried any real threat in front of goal. It was Brown who completed the tale of woe for his home-town side when he scored a rather streaky fifth in off the crossbar near the end – but by then all the interest had long, long gone.

Entertainment: 7

Swindon: Downsborough; Dawson, Trollope; Morgan, Nurse, Shergold; Weaver, Brown, Lawton, Smart, Rogers.

Reading: Dixon; Meldrum, Evans; Cook, Thornhill, Travers; Knight, Allen, Terry, McDonald, Webb.

Referee: J. Osborne (Ipswich)

With Hunt and Summerbee now gone, Don was the undoubted star of the Swindon side, and the scouts continued to flock to the County Ground to check his performances. It was only a matter of time before a big club came calling. This duly happened in the autumn and the club was Liverpool, the FA Cup holders, who were building a formidable side under the management of Bill Shankly. The board turned the approach down:

> I remember the Liverpool approach – but I knew no more than anybody else – I read about it in the papers. The club said nothing to me, back then it was very different, if the club didn't want you to leave then they had all the power – not like today. Some people said I had no ambition, but it wasn't that, I couldn't do anything about leaving, and anyway I was very happy at Swindon – I was in the first team, and scoring goals, what more can you want?

John Trollope knew his old friend was a wanted man:

> In those days nearly every week there was something in the papers about Don and clubs being interested. I think Wolves were very keen as well as Liverpool, and maybe one or two of the London clubs. I remember our old trainer, Harry Cousins, a man who used to say in two words what some people said in twenty, saying to Don before kick-offs: 'There's someone here to watch you today, Don' to encourage him to put on a show – not that he needed much encouragement mind.

To return to the subject of Liverpool, does Don wish now that he had gone?

> Not really, because I enjoyed my career and my time at Swindon. I had a great rapport with the fans, and of course the side ultimately became very successful. Of course, it does occasionally go through your mind about what might have happened if I had moved on, but there is no guarantee that it would have all worked out.

Keith Morgan thinks Don should have gone:

> I think Liverpool would have been a great move for him, and I do think that overall he stayed at Swindon too long. He was a big fish in a small pond. Had he gone earlier I think he would have been an England regular. I can understand him not wanting to move though, because we were a real family club: on a Saturday night, all the players at the club – first team, reserves, A team – went out together, all fifty or so players.

In retrospect, 1965/66 was a very important season in the Don story. His new manager was building a side that would put Don in the national limelight, he had discovered the art of goalscoring, and he had shown that the early promise was going to be fulfilled.

By the end of the season, Don was not just Swindon's star player, but he was also an England Under-23 international – some achievement for a player plying his trade in the Third Division – and he was still only twenty-one. The future looked bright.

Goalscorer Supreme

In the next three seasons, 1966/67, 1967/68 and 1968/69, Don would score over 90 goals, a quite remarkable total for a winger, and one that made him one of the highest scorers anywhere in the country over that period. Football in those days was becoming a different game. The old 'WM' formation (2-3-5 in today's terms), with two full-backs, three wing halves (or half-backs), and five forwards (two wingers, two inside forwards and a centre forward), was being phased out. This change was accelerated by England's World Cup win in the summer of 1966, which was achieved by playing a 4-4-2 formation... with no wingers.

Don remembers that Swindon had no such thing as a fixed formation: 'We had a very flexible formation back then. One week it was 4-2-4, and then it would be 4-5-1. In fact we would often change during a game, depending on what was happening in the match.'

John Trollope also recalls the formations back then: 'Looking back on it, I guess it was more about a "W" than an "M" formation – although the back four were quite fixed, the front six were very flexible. Really we only played one out-and-out striker, so we needed midfielders to come forward and Don was absolutely key in that respect.'

So why was it that Don scored so many goals?

I think part of it was that people were saying to me, don't come back into defence, because you're a liability – you stay in the opponents' half. It does help you when you don't have to worry about coming back: all you are focused on is scoring or creating goals. We were a good side, partly because we played to our own strengths, and mine was obviously attacking. Confidence obviously had a lot to do with scoring goals, especially when you were one-on-one with the goalkeeper, and I got a lot that way down the years, particularly in these seasons we're talking about.

My own playing days, other than the odd five-a-side, are now a thing of the past, so Don's tips to me on how to score goals one-on one are a bit academic. For other readers, they may be a bit more relevant:

The thing about going one-on-one with the goalkeeper is that often you have a while to think about it. I always believed that if you were running at the goalkeeper from a long way out, then you should try and go round the goalkeeper, whereas for one-on-ones close in you should just knock it past them. I think most people would say that.

John Trollope has his own view:

The best two one-on-one finishers I have ever seen were Don and Jimmy Greaves. Don scored lots of goals that way. He had the confidence to dip his shoulder and go round the goalkeeper – a bit like the third goal at Wembley. If he saw a gap he used to cut inside and go for goal. The number of goals he scored was fantastic really, because remember he was a winger, and wingers were supposed to be there to cross the ball for centre forwards to score! Mind you, he made lots of goals as well – he always saw the wider situation. Some players overdo the dribbling, but Don was able to see what was needed in any situation and bring other players into the game if that was what was best for the team.

Part of the reason for the goalscoring record was the fact that Don was now playing in what was a free-scoring side, particularly at home. In both the 1966/67 and 1967/68 seasons, the side managed over 50 home League goals, and in both seasons the side was the third-highest scoring team in the division. Yet despite those statistics, they 'only' finished seventh, and then tenth in those two seasons.

So was there frustration that the goals didn't take Swindon up? Don recalls:

> I think most teams went out there to score goals. I know we did, and at the risk of sounding blasé, we were only interested in scoring more than the opposition. In fact, even the year we went up (1968/69), two of the games I remember were a 6-2 win at Northampton and a 5-3 win at Tranmere – there's five goals conceded in two games, but we'd scored eleven! We knew we had to tighten up defensively, and we did get better and better – and if you think ahead to the cup-winning side, then that had a great defence with Rod Thomas, Frank Burrows, Stan Harland and John Trollope – a great back four, and of course a goalkeeper who could save anything in Peter Downsborough.

In the end, it was tightening up the defence that made the difference. After a goals against figure of 59 in 1966/67 and 51 in 1967/68, only 35 goals were conceded in the promotion season of 1968/69. But we jump ahead of ourselves.

Back to the summer of 1966. After getting used to life back in the Third Division in the previous season, and adjusting to the departures of Hunt and Summerbee, there were high hopes that Swindon might challenge for a return to the Second Division. Don recalls being cautiously optimistic, as the saying goes: 'I think we knew we were getting better. Each year we thought we had more of a chance as Danny Williams developed the team. For 1966 I think we were still a bit short, but we knew we'd score goals so we were still hopeful.'

Those hopes would be dashed early. Only one of the first eleven matches would be won, and, after a 4-0 defeat at Middlesbrough on 15 October, Town had just five points from those games and were in deep trouble. A 1-1 draw at Walsall in the next game, with Don scoring his third goal of the season, set them on a better run. Don remembers this as a pivotal game:

> Walsall was a really important game for us that season. We went up there for a night match and got a 1-1 draw. I can remember that as clear as day. We played very well and we should have won. We came back into the dressing room and thought we were unlucky not to win, and suddenly we realised that we could still play and were a good team, despite the start.

The next ten games saw seven wins and only one defeat, and included another Don hat-trick, this time in the 6-3 home win over Oldham Athletic on 3 December. Don had forgotten this achievement: 'Did I really score a hat-trick against Oldham. Sorry, can't remember it at all. And 6-3 too, must have been some game – just shows, doesn't it, how you can remember some games so well, and forget others!' Just to prove it, here is the match report.

ROGERS STARS AS SWINDON SLAM SIX

by James Hastings

Swindon 6 Oldham 3

When bustling Frank Large nodded the ball past Peter Downsborough to open the scoring against his old colleagues in the 10th minute, the odds looked very much on Oldham strengthening their challenge to the top sides.

For in the opening spell, Swindon had looked all at sea against Oldham's accurate push-and-run attack, and the defence was getting in all sorts of tangles.

But Swindon gradually worked their way back, and the reliable and talented Don Rogers laid-on an equaliser in the 18th minute. His cross from the by-line was side-footed out by Jim Bowie, but Swindon's leading marksman Dennis Brown hammered it into the net from the edge of the penalty area.

Seven minutes later, Rogers stepped in again. He chased a long ball from Bruce Walker, which the Oldham defenders seemed not to be interested in. With superb control and coolness, Rogers dribbled inside, went round goal-keeper Ron Swan, and shot into the net.

The second half began with a flourish. Reg Blore sent a shot inches wide, but in the 50th minute Rogers stood unruffled and prodded in Swindon's third goal from Walker's cross. Then Swindon hit twice in two minutes. In the 66th minute, Brown hit home a glorious low drive from Willie Penman's pass, and Walker turned in a fifth, again from Rogers' pass.

But Oldham were not finished, and when John Collins flicked in a goal from a corner in the 79th minute, they found a new lease of life. Two minutes later Ian Towers smacked in Oldham's third, and Swindon's winning lead began to look in danger.

Oldham's pressure led to their undoing once more in the 87th minute. The irrepressible Rogers whipped across another pinpoint centre, Smart headed the ball goalwards, and Rogers danced in to make sure.

It was just reward for the most accomplished footballer on the field. A last-minute thrill came when Swindon right-back Rod Thomas hooked clear from under his own crossbar.

Yet this was a season where the only consistent things about the team was their inconsistency. The next six games were all lost, with a run of four successive games in which the team didn't score (remember this was the side that finished third-top scorers in the division). After a 3-1 defeat at Shrewsbury, they were back in trouble. Don laughs now at the inconsistency, although I suspect that neither he nor his team-mates were doing so at the time: 'What a mixed-up season that was. We were great for a period and then terrible for a spell. It was so up and down. I don't think any of us knew why, because we were clearly a very good side.'

The season was rescued by a great run in the FA Cup, a run that was to feature some of Don's greatest performances for Swindon, and once more draw national attention to his talents. Don scored in both of the first two rounds, matches that were won comfortably against non-League opposition. That took Swindon into the third round, and another match against West Ham United, the side who had knocked them out of both FA and League Cups two years previously.

This was a massive draw. West Ham were one of the glamour clubs of the time, not only because of their recent run of success (FA Cup winners in 1964, European Cup Winners' Cup winners in 1965 and League Cup winners in 1966), but because they had three of the key members of the England World Cup-winning team – the two goalscorers in the World Cup final, Geoff Hurst and Martin Peters, together with the England captain, Bobby Moore.

Few gave Swindon a chance, although Maurice Golesworthy, previewing the match in the football weekly *Soccer Star*, noted that 'in football anything can happen in the Cup and West Ham will need to keep a careful eye on their visitors' outside-right, for Don Rogers at his best is capable of rattling any defence.'

In the event, the tie at Upton Park produced a 3-3 draw. As the report shows, it was a thrilling game. Mattick also quotes the *News of the World* reporter Peter Morehead on the game: 'Swindon were magnificent! They outplayed, outfought and outgunned West Ham in everything but goals in the Upton Park mud.'

They so nearly created an upset. After twice trailing to goals by Geoff Hurst, Don scored his second goal of the game to give Swindon the lead for the first time, only for Hurst to complete his hat-trick. It had been a magnificent performance and Don had been at the heart of it, although, typically, he prefers to dwell on the game:

What a cup-tie that was – one of the best games I ever played in. It was great. They were a superb side, of course, but we matched them and we could have won. I can still remember Geoff Hurst scoring the equaliser near the end. The famous photograph was taken in that game – Bobby Moore pulling my shirt, which people still talk to me about.

DON ROGERS- WHAT A DAZZLER

by Sam Bartram,
(News of the World)

West Ham United 3   Swindon Town 3

Geoff Hurst, England's World Cup hero, had to produce another hat-trick to save West Ham's FA Cup life against Third Division Swindon. But not even Hurst was the man of this stirring match. That accolade goes to Don Rogers, of Swindon. Liverpool and Arsenal are after him. I don't blame them.

Swindon manager Danny Williams told me: 'Bill Shankly is on the 'phone every other week wanting to sign the boy, but wants him for peanuts. I reckon he must be worth £80,000 so I say "No".'

And I don't blame Williams for that. This kid, yesterday, was worth every pound, shilling and pence any club could raise. He scored twice and made the other Swindon goal for Brown. And in between he tormented, terrified and tanned the football out of a team London reckons is a match for the best in the world.

Full-back Bovington has faced the great names of Europe – but I'll wager he has never met a man of Rogers' talents. Nor have his team-mates – Bobby Moore and Martin Peters among them – seen many who could dominate a match so effectively.

He needed support, of course. And he got it. Swindon matched West Ham for skill in every department. The defence gave little away and when West Ham did get through. their efforts were usually foiled by brilliant goalkeeper Hicks.

Swindon also lasted better in the muddy conditions – despite West Ham's policy of swinging the ball about whenever possible. This paid off for the first goal. Sealey sent Brabrook away and the winger's cross was confidently hit in by Hurst. It paid again after Rogers had fired Swindon level as Hurst brilliantly headed West Ham's second.

Rogers had a long cross gathered by Standen. He just finger-tipped another shot by the winger round a post.

West Ham were not wasting time. Hicks had to save from Dear and Hurst, but it was no surprise when Rogers laid on the chance for Brown to equalise after 15 minutes of the second half. Two more brilliant saves from Standen – one dive to the feet of Rogers and a staggering stop from Brown – kept eager Swindon out until the 72nd minute.

Then Rogers took the ball downfield and fired past an astonished Standen with all the confidence in the world. West Ham can rarely have been more surprised. Credit them for keeping their heads, building attacks with calm assurance, and having their reward when Hurst headed the blush-saver 12 minutes from the end.

They live to fight again on Tuesday – but I've a feeling that even West Ham, the best soccer thinkers in the country, will still be wondering how to stop tearaway Rogers.

The replay was at the County Ground three days later in front of over 25,000. This time the Robins won, goals by Don and Ken Skeen in the last six minutes sealing their victory. It remains one of the greatest cup wins in the club's history. Don wasn't surprised:

> It sounds a bit arrogant, but we really fancied our chances in the replay. We'd given them a really good game up there, and probably should have won, and thought that we could beat them in front of our own fans. In the end we beat them quite convincingly I thought.

Maurice Weedon, writing in *Soccer Star*, was very clear about Swindon's star man:

After Swindon had pulled off one of the biggest shocks in the FA Cup for many years by drawing 3-3 at West Ham, the player who was the centre of conversation amongst the 37,000 spectators was Don Rogers, Swindon's twenty-one-year-old outside-left, and with good reason, for he had a wonderful match. He tore the Hammers defence to shreds, and even such experienced men as Martin Peters, Bobby Moore and Eddie Bovington could not contain him. Rogers scored twice and laid on the third... undoubtedly the match belonged to Rogers. West Ham fans were confident that their side could turn the tables in the replay saying: 'They'll hold Rogers next time'. But it was as impossible as it is to hold water in your hand... with six minutes left Rogers pulled off another master stroke. Receiving the ball, he went straight towards goal, shot on the run and restored Swindon's lead.

Clive King, the long-standing reporter who covered the Town for many years as a journalist on the *Evening Advertiser*, wrote in his match report of the replay, under the heading 'Rogers brilliant': '... and once again the Hammers had no answer to left-winger Rogers. He was constantly a thorn in their flesh, and his pace from a standing start had to be seen at times to be believed.'

The fourth round saw Swindon beat Second Division Bury 2-1 at home, with Don scoring again, which meant that he had scored in every round so far. Next up were Nottingham Forest, another strong First Division side (they would finish runners-up to Manchester United at the end of the season). Once again Swindon were magnificent: after a 0-0 draw away in the first game, followed by a 1-1 draw in the replay, they were only beaten at the third time of asking, 3-0 (all the goals in the second half) in a second replay at Villa Park, in front of over 52,000. Again Don was the star man:

We should have won at Forest – I missed a one-on-one, which if I'd taken, we would have won. Then of course, Bruce Walker scored a thirty-yarder at Swindon to equalise right near the end, to take us to Villa Park. That was some night – a massive crowd – I'd never played in front of anything like that. With hindsight though, we'd missed our chance in the first match – I know that I said we thought we'd beat West Ham in the replay, but usually you don't play two games against better sides where you can match them all the time. I think it's still the same today.

Keith Morgan can remember the game well:

Forest away was the only one-on-one I ever saw Don miss. It was in the last minute as well, and I can remember when we saw him through we thought we were going to win. To be fair he was very unlucky – he went past the goalkeeper, but the 'keeper just stuck out a leg and the ball went out for a corner.

John Trollope recalls:

Forest were a really good side then and we gave them three really good games. I remember a lot of people got locked out at Villa Park; the Swindon supporters always enjoyed the cup, dressing up as Moonrakers and the like. We were always known as a cup side, and we always seemed to do well against the bigger clubs, with Don normally at the centre of what we did.

The cup run not only boosted the club's finances off the pitch, but also had a positive impact on the pitch as well. From the end of February to the season's finish in mid-May they played a further 18 League games (nine of them in April alone, as they caught up on a fixture list disrupted by the FA Cup run), and won twelve (including seven games in succession), drew four and lost only two. It was promotion, indeed Championship, form, but came much too late, and the final position was eighth. Don is philosophical:

As I said, it was a crazy season really – the cup run shows just how good we were when we played well, and that run at the end of the season was great – we couldn't do anything wrong. Mind you, there was no pressure, because we knew we weren't going up or down, but it still shows that it was a very good team.

For Don it had been a fantastic campaign. He had played in every one of Swindon's 59 League and cup matches that season, and had scored 32 goals – an incredible tally.

I think it was one of my best seasons for the club, because the side wasn't as strong as it was later on, so to score 32 goals, thinking about it now, was tremendous really. I don't think that I'd say it was as good as 1968/69 though, because there was nothing at the end of the season – you remember things more when you win something.

Most of those goals came running through the middle; I didn't get any with my head. I think I was past that stage by then. I still get stick about my lack of headed goals even now, and I just say, what's the game called? Football! In fact, in my defence I could head a ball all right, it's just I never got in the position to score with my head.

Don's lack of headed goals was a constant source of amusement to his teammates. Frank Burrows was very keen that his assessment of Don's heading ability should be included in this book… 'The one thing we all enjoyed was watching Don trying to head a ball – this big six-foot player attempting to score with his head – he would run a mile to avoid having to head the ball! In all the time I played with him, I don't think I ever saw him score with his head.'

Heading ability or not, it had been an excellent season, as John Trollope, who played with Don for ten seasons is happy to confirm: 'I think Don's performances that year were on a par with 1968/69 when he got all the publicity. It was a great season, and he was at his very best.'

The national press had taken note, mainly due to the performances of Don during the cup run. Here is Maurice Weedon again:

> Rogers is a colourful player, and when the ball goes in his direction
> a buzz of expectancy vibrates around the ground, for he is always
> likely to pull off some stroke of football magic which lifts the game
> to a fever-pitch of excitement. Although he fills the outside left
> position, he is liable to pop up anywhere to start an attack, and is
> very much a two-footed player; being equally at home on the
> right-wing or in the middle as he is on the left-wing.
>
> Now that Rogers has 'arrived' as far as the press are concerned,
> he will start receiving the praise he deserves. Not that being over-
> looked in the past has worried him. He is a very modest youngster
> who has never been concerned about it. He loves football and
> gives his best for the whole 90 minutes of the match.

There is often a trend that how a club finishes one season has a
major impact on how they will do in the following campaign.
Clubs that finish poorly cannot regain confidence; by contrast,
clubs that end on a high note can often carry that momentum over
to the following season. Given that trend, then the players and
management must have been very confident about 1967/68.
Don comments:

> We were building a very good side by then. Most of the team who
> won promotion were with us by then (in fact only Frank Burrows
> of the following seasons regular side didn't play that season). We
> had some new players in, and we did fancy our chances. Peter
> Noble came that year – he was a great signing for us (although it
> doesn't stop another Don anecdote about how he could never
> understand the Geordie striker's accent) – a superb header of the
> ball for his size and a real trier.

In the event, as in 1966/67, they got off to a slow start with fifteen
points from the first fifteen matches – respectable, but not promo-

tion form. Don was among the goals again with eight strikes over that period, but at the age of twenty-two he was now starting to realise, that, for the sake of his career, he might have to leave. In November 1967 he submitted a transfer request: 'Rogers Tells Swindon: Sell Me NOW' was one newspaper headline.

The situation regarding a player's contract was somewhat different then. There was no such thing as a 'Bosman' and it was the clubs, not the players who held the upper hand. Essentially, clubs had to agree to player's requests for transfers; at the end of one contract, provided that the club offered the same amount of money, then the player was obliged to re-sign. With no pressing financial need to sell, Swindon were adamant that their star player was going nowhere... and there was nothing he could do about it.

> I must have been unhappy about something – probably the fact that we hadn't started so well, and I couldn't see us gaining promotion. I was always happy to stay at Swindon if we were progressing as a club, but I did want to play at a higher level. Although I had been tapped up in the past, I wasn't then, I probably got some more money out of it though – that's what used to happen when I indicated I wasn't happy, not that money really bothered me, because if had, I would have moved.

John Trollope didn't blame his good friend for asking for a transfer:

> I don't think we were that surprised by Don's transfer request – although we all took it that the club looked after him on the money side as a result – in those days nobody knew what everybody else was on. I think we all accepted though that the best players would be on the best money.

So what went on then? Contemporary reports, again from *Soccer Star*, indicate that the bids were coming in at around the £100,000 mark, which the magazine described as a ludicrous amount for someone unproven at the highest level. Here is Brian Marshall, writing in early December 1967: 'As I write Wolves have already put in an offer in writing while Spurs have also entered the market. With such clubs willing to through their caps into the ring, the stakes will be high, and Swindon will not miss any opportunity to take any club to the limit.'

In fact the situation was thus: Wolves offered £90,000 (or to be more precise, goalkeeper Fred Davies plus £70,000). To put this in context, the record transfer fee for a winger at that stage was £80,000. Besides Spurs, the other clubs who were interested were West Bromwich Albion, Nottingham Forest (who of course had seen Don at close quarters the season before), West Ham (likewise), and Stoke City. In addition, the Swindon chairman, Wilf Castle, commented that 'quite a number of clubs let it be known that they would be interested if we had decided to sell'. In a later profile of Don, done by the *Evening Advertiser* in 1995, the final total of clubs who expressed an interest in him at this time was given as eighteen.

SWINDON TO KEEP ROGERS

Decision of the Town FC board is unanimous

by Clive King
(Evening Advertiser)

Swindon Town's directors decided unanimously last night that the transfer request of England under-23 winger, Don Rogers, should not be granted. This decision was made public by Mr W.J. Castle, Chairman of the Board, after he had broken the news to Rogers this morning. 'We looked at the position from every angle and came to the conclusion after long deliberation. We feel that our decision was honestly in the interests of the club' added the chairman. Mr Castle then emphasised that the board's decision was not tied up with any offers that Swindon had received. 'They were not even considered' he said.

Mr Castle's announcement ended a week of speculation which followed a £70,000 plus goalkeeper Fred Davies bid by Wolverhampton Wanderers.

This was immediately followed by Rogers making his request for a transfer because he wanted First Division football. Since then the story has become the centre of countless newspaper reports and television interviews with prospective fees as high as £100,000 placed on the twenty-two- year-old winger's head.

The decision to keep Rogers can now really only mean one thing- that the board are determined in their bid to bring a return of Second Division football to Swindon. Rogers, who has a two-year contract, with another year optional, has stated that he has no argument with the club, other than the fact that he feels he would like First Division football. Only by making a rapid bid for promotion can the directors therefore please both club and player.

Invited to comment on the board's decision, Don Rogers said 'It will not make any difference to the way I feel. I am still extremely determined to get away and shall be seeing Mr Williams (the Town manager) as soon as possible.'

It is worth reflecting on this episode in Don's career. One of the biggest criticisms he received during his career (and indeed since it ended) was that he lacked ambition, and was content to let his talents go to waste in a lower division. Although he was later to withdraw his request, there is no doubt that he was very keen to get away at this stage. This is clearly at odds with the image traditionally portrayed. Indeed, as we shall see, by the time he finally left Swindon, he would have asked on four separate occasions to go. His essentially loyal nature meant that he didn't create a huge fuss when his requests were turned down, but don't overlook the drive to better himself that was there when he felt Swindon couldn't help him achieve his personal ambitions.

Although frustrating for Don, there is much to admire about the club's decision not to sell him, at least from a fan's perspective. At the heart of the club's decision not to sell was a worry that any sale would be seen as a 'breach of faith with supporters' − in the summer they had sold season tickets (£17,000 worth, an excellent return in those days), on the basis that Don would not be transferred. Indeed, a group of season-ticket holders went to see the board asking if they would get their money back in the event of a sale once news of Don's request became public. Mr Castle announced the club's decision like this, describing it as 'one of the most difficult problems the club has ever faced' and stated that 'We have acted in a way which we think best for the club and our supporters. Naturally the money would have come in useful – what Third Division club couldn't do with £100,000, but there is more to it than that.'

It is perhaps worth digressing a little, to talk about Don's personal situation. Clearly he was coveted by major clubs. In those days, as indeed today, any player who could score with the frequency that Don did, not to mention the other goals he created, would be extremely valuable. There will always be some debate about whether a player from the Third Division can make the jump up into a higher league, but in this instance surely there was limited risk – Don had played, and done well in the Second Division, he had shone in cup matches against First Division sides, and had also gained international recognition. Remember too, that this was in an era where far more players did move from lower division clubs into the First Division: the top clubs in the 1960s didn't simply go out and sign a major international star from abroad (or some untried Eastern European centre forward on the basis of an agent's video).

I know there were lots of offers for me, but you only found out through the press, or when people told you a long time after the event. We've already talked about Liverpool wanting to sign me, Wolves were very keen too, and then I know later on from Malcolm Allison that Joe Mercer tried to sign me for Manchester City. I am sure there were others but the club never told me. In those days, the clubs held all the power – if you were under contract they didn't have to tell you.

Don is philosophical now; back in 1967/68, he was less than thrilled that the club wouldn't sell him, as was evident from an article in *Jimmy Hill's Football Weekly* in March 1968. Despite the fact that his transfer request had been refused he still wanted to get away and was quoted as saying 'I want First Division football and I think I deserve the chance to make the grade in it. It's not a question of money, just one of ambition.'

One amusing part of the article was Bertie Mee, the Arsenal manager, questioning whether Don was 'consistent enough' for the First Division. Arsenal at one stage had been interested enough to make a firm offer – this was at the start of the previous season – of an undisclosed fee plus Alan Skirton. Now Bertie Mee had changed his mind and commented 'We have had him watched many times and our conclusion is that he is not consistent enough, particularly away from home.' Twelve months later, Don would give Mee the chance to see at first hand whether this was a fair view to hold…

Given the fact that clubs held the power, one way round this was for the unscrupulous practice of 'tapping', whereby a club approached a player without telling the team he played for, and tried to set up a move that way by getting the player to agitate for a transfer. Although it was illegal, everybody knew it went on. Don was no exception to this practice:

> I was only tapped up once in my career – fairly early on. I'm not going to say who the club was, because I don't want anyone to get into trouble, but it was a high profile First Division club. Nothing came of it because Swindon wouldn't sell anyway.

John Trollope was a little surprised that Don didn't move on earlier:

> I think everybody expected that Don would move on really, and perhaps if he had done a bit earlier he might have done better. I still think he was one of the best wide players never to get a full international cap, and he might have done so had he left the club before he did.

So Swindon kept their star player, and briefly it looked as if they might be able to capitalise by making a real push for promotion. Don scored five goals in seven games in the run-up to Christmas, by which time they were just two points behind the leaders. Four points in two games against Torquay, who were then in second place, meant that the team ended the year in third place – a point behind the Devon side, and two points behind leaders Walsall.

> The game I remember in that good run was Reading at home. They absolutely murdered us in the first half, and we came off either nil-nil or one down. Then in the second half we scored early and we annihilated them and won 5-1. Talk about a game of two halves – this was definitely one of them.

Momentum was affected by poor weather and another good cup run, which meant that only five League matches (two wins, three defeats) took place between the end of December and the end of February. This left sixteen matches – over a third of the season – still to be played in the last ten weeks of the season; of these only four were won, to leave the team well off the pace in tenth position.

The FA Cup, as in the previous season, offered some respite. Second Division Blackburn were beaten at the County Ground in the third round, to take the Robins through to a fourth-round tie at First Division Sheffield Wednesday. Roger Smart gave them a first-half lead, but despite another good performance against higher division opposition, the team lost 2-1, with the winner coming five minutes from time.

Don doesn't have fond memories of the game

> We should have won that one. We were the better side. I missed a couple that day that I should have scored. The thing is, I doubt you'll find any mention of that in the match report – people didn't write bad things about me at that stage – when you get in with the press and you're doing well, all they want to write is good things, and then when things don't go so well, all they write are bad

things. Sometimes I used to look in *The People* on a Sunday and see I was the star man, and I'd wonder what they were on about – I'd only had two kicks of the ball, and I'd get eight out of ten. It was all about what they think you were like, rather than what you'd done on the day. Embarrassing really.

So another season petered out. The problem wasn't in the goalscoring stakes, or in the home form, where only two games were lost. The two factors that cost a higher position, and possibly promotion were the age-old bugbears of the 'away wins' column (only three all season), and a new issue – the number of draws. Swindon drew seventeen games during the season (the highest number of draws since entering the League back in 1921). For Don, it had not been quite the season he was hoping the team would have 'It was all a bit disappointing with all the draws, although on the positive side, we were definitely getting harder to beat.'

Don had again done his bit, and more. The 25 League goals he contributed was his highest tally during his time at Swindon, and he had now not missed a League or cup game since April 1964. It was all very frustrating:

I had a lot of people, local people, asking me what I was doing, staying at Swindon, because I was scoring a lot of goals, and still creating them as well. But I was very happy, I was scoring goals and playing in a team I could see was getting better, and that mattered a lot.

Don needed something to reignite his career. Fortunately for all concerned, that something was just round the corner.

The Wembley Wizard

Manager Danny Williams had now been at Swindon for three seasons, during which time the team had flattered to deceive. They were capable of outstanding free-scoring football at times, but inconsistent, particularly away from home, with a tendency to concede too many goals. To try and help work on the 'goals against' column, Williams signed Frank Burrows, a tall, commanding centre half from Scunthorpe. With Mel Nurse moving on to Swansea, Stan Harland, who was to be Burrows' regular partner at the heart of the defence, took over the captaincy.

In fact the team was not much changed for the 1968/69 season. True, Burrows had signed, as had midfielder John Smith and striker Chris Jones (although Jones was to have a limited impact), but other than them the team remained the same. Nevertheless, something had changed, recalls Don:

> You always hope it will be your year of course, and I think there are cycles in football, so every ten years or so most clubs will have a good year – they do well in the League or have a good cup run. We knew we were getting better, and I think the signing of Frank Burrows was very important because he completed what was a great defence – and our success that season was very much based

on the fact that we were so good at the back – for most successful teams that's the case. If you look at our regular back four, then Rod Thomas and Stan Harland went on to play in the First Division, and there's no doubt that John Trollope and Frank Burrows could have played at that level as well. Their tackling was very strong, and they were all very good in the air. Peter Downsborough was a superb 'keeper as well – a very good shot-stopper.

Frank Burrows says that he knew all about the star winger of the team he was joining:

> I'd played against Don when I was at Scunthorpe. We had a full-back called Derek Hemstead, a good strong player, and our manager was Freddie Goodwin, who used to play for Manchester United and Leeds United. He was a young manager then, and he had us very well organised. Anyway, Freddie said to Derek, show Don Rogers inside, he's not so good when you show him inside. So Derek duly did this, and Don cut inside past him, so I was the next man. I went to close him down and, as I did so, he had a shot from about thirty yards, just before I got to him, which hit the bar and rebounded back off over my head towards the centre circle. So I turned to Derek and said, 'If that's his bad side, I wouldn't want to see his good side!

During the period 1986 to 1996, Swindon had some memorable times - two League titles, and three play-off triumphs, one of which led to a first, and so far only, spell in the top flight of English football. However, it is the 1968/69 season that most fans would choose as the greatest in the history of the club.

From early on, it was evident that the 'goals against' column would show an improvement – no side scored against Swindon in the first six matches. That period was also notable because, in the second game of the season, at Hartlepool, Don was missing through injury. This was the first time he had missed a Swindon first-team fixture for 206 games. John Trollope recalls that day with a rueful smile:

That was the first game that Don had missed for a while, and I remember I broke my arm. Don didn't travel north, and when we came back he told me 'Look what happens to you when I'm not there to protect you'. To be fair to Don, I hadn't realised that he had so many consecutive games – quite an achievement for a winger who was being clattered: it was easier for us full-backs who were doing the clattering!

John, modest man that he is, is of course being a little self-deprecating, not just by portraying full-backs in the way he does, but also by not drawing attention to the fact that in each of those 206 games he had been at left-back and in fact the injury brought to an end an even more impressive run of games than Don – 368 to be precise.

So the team was unbeaten in the first six matches, and although successive away defeats in the next two games raised some concerns, a run of seven straight wins gave notice that the team were going to be a real challenger for promotion. The last of these games was at home to Southport on 2 November 1968. A crowd of 18,913 saw the Town win 5-1, which included four goals from everyone's favourite winger.

ROGERS A FOUR-GOAL SMASHER

by Gerald Cook

Swindon 5 Southport 1

Wonderful Don Rogers. The Swindon star smashed four goals in the thrashing of Southport. Nearly 19,000 gave Swindon's cup fighters a rousing reception and in turn were treated to some great goals. There were some surprising scores too, with a couple of goals which looked offside.

But it was the Rogers show which overshadowed everything else. He was always too speedy for the Southport's defenders, who rarely knew where to find him and his shooting accuracy made scoring look simple.

Rogers netted his first goal in the 22nd minute when he suddenly turned up on the right to glide easily past Andy Clarke, and beat John Armstrong from a narrow angle.

There were one or two long-range efforts by Southport's Terry Harkin and Eric Redrobe before Rogers notched his second in the 32nd minute. This time he looked to be well offside when he took Roger Smart's pass, but the winger did not hesitate and again Armstrong was left helpless.

Southport's best effort before the interval came from Tony Crossley. He dribbled in from the left, evading a couple of tackles before smashing the ball inches over the bar.

Swindon lost Willie Penman after 30 minutes, and Chris Jones substituted, while just before the interval Redrobe was led off with a gashed head which required three stitches and Tony Field took his place.

John Smith, a tremendous worker in midfield for Swindon, combined well with Jones to score Swindon's third goal in the 47th minute. After this Swindon seemed inclined to take a breather and allowed Southport to come back into the game. Colin Alty urged his colleagues forward, and Harkin was unlucky with a good effort which scraped the bar.

But in the 68th minute George Andrews reduced Southport's arrears when everybody expected him to be pulled up for offside. In the next minute or two Downsborough twice made desperate clearances, but Swindon soon took control again. In the 82nd minute Stan Harland forsook his sweeper role to join the attack and was only pulled down a yard or two from goal. Rogers stroked home the penalty kick and in injury time the left-winger added his fourth goal when he once more left the Southport defence standing to finish with a great shot.

Swindon: Downsborough, Dawson, Thomas, Penman, Burrows, Harland, Heath, Noble, Smith, Smart, Rogers. Sub: Jones

Southport: Armstrong, Pearson, Clarke, Peat, Russell (M), Alty, Shaw, Andrews, Redrobe, Harkin, Crossley. Sub: Field

It says much for Don's genuinely modest character that, as was often the case during our conversations, he looks at me in stunned silence when I remind him of some major personal achievement…

I scored four goals against Southport? I don't remember that –they must have been a poor side!' Then his memory does kick in, but of another game against the same side: 'I do remember Southport away – we drew 1-1 and I remember my goal, it was a tap-in from four or five yards – someone had a shot and the 'keeper parried it to me. I think I remember that goal because I didn't score many like that.

Meanwhile, another cup run was developing, this time in the League Cup. By the time Don scored his quartet of goals at the start of November the team were into the quarter-finals – the furthest they had ever gone in the competition, and the best cup run for the club since the days of Harold Fleming and the cup fighters of the early 1900s. Wins over Torquay United, Bradford City, (after a replay) – although 'Bradford very nearly beat us in both matches' says Frank Burrows – and Second Division Blackburn Rovers, took them through to another cup match against a top-flight club – their eighth cup tie (including replays) against a First Division side in two years. The side they faced were Coventry City, and over 3,000 Swindon fans made the relatively short trip to Highfield Road. They nearly saw a major upset, as their side, with Don outstanding,outplayed Coventry to lead 2-0 with four minutes remaining, before the home side struck back to earn what the local paper, *The Coventry Evening Telegraph*, described as 'a lucky replay'.

Don would agree with their view:

We were absolutely strolling the game with ten minutes to go and my wife and father-in-law left early to beat the traffic, because they thought we'd won it. They stopped half an hour down the road on the way home to have a drink and only then did they hear that it was 2-2. That was really where the cup run started – we played very well, and they didn't look like scoring a goal against us. We should have won, no doubt about it.

The replay took place five days later on 21 October. This time Swindon made no mistake, winning 3-0, with all the goals coming in the first half. Don was again instrumental in the win, setting up goals two and three, and, as he had done at Highfield Road in the first game, scoring his side's first goal, which the *Evening Advertiser* described like this:

> After a Coventry attack had been broken up in the tenth minute, Town struck back quickly with a counter-move. The ball went clear to Thomas near the left wing, and the full-back slipped it inside to Rogers. For a split-second the City defenders seemed mesmerised as they sensed the imminent danger – and Rogers seemed to be the only player not moving in slow motion. The Swindon player moved the ball onto his right foot before unleashing a bomb-like drive which 'exploded' into the net behind the despairingly groping hands of City goalkeeper Glazier.

All the headlines after the game were made by Don: 'Rogers sets Swindon on glory trail' and 'Rogers' skill crushes Coventry' being two of them. The man himself says it was comfortable in the end:

> We were much better than them – quite an achievement for a Third Division side against a First Division side – we played very well, and it was comfortable really. Those two games were very important in the context of the season, because it made us realise how good we were.

Next up were Derby County, a side, who, under the management of the late, legendary Brian Clough, would gain promotion to the First Division at the end of the season. Once more Swindon were drawn away. By now cup fever had gripped the town and the travelling Swindon contingent was up to 7,000. They saw a thrilling game which ended goal-less, although Don was described as 'wasting the best opportunity of the entire 90 minutes' by the *Derby Evening Telegraph*. To be fair to him, he had made the chance himself, cutting through the middle of the pitch before firing over the bar. All he can remember though is what his thoughts were coming off the pitch: 'I think it was then that I thought we might be destined to win the cup. We got annihilated. They were far better than us, and did everything but score: it was like the Alamo at our goal.' When we came off we thought "Crikey, we were lucky there!"'

The replay was played on Bonfire Night, three days after Don had scored his four goals against Southport. Nearly 27,000 were at the County Ground to see the home side reach the semi-finals with a 1-0 win. Don scored the only goal and generally ran amok. The team from the Third Division were through to the semi-final.

> We were lucky against them at home as well really. The goal went in off Dave Mackay's back and looped over the 'keeper – I think you'd say I was credited it with it rather than I scored it. Nine times out of ten, it would probably have looped over the bar, but this time it went in. The key though was our defence; to keep two clean sheets against a side of the quality of Derby was some achievement for them – and indeed all the side, not just the back four and the 'keeper. People like Joe Butler did a lot of defending, so did Don Heath, and Roger Smart was up and down like a yo-yo.

Just over two weeks later, the first leg of the semi-final took place. Town's opponents were Burnley, then an established First Division side, with the first leg at Turf Moor. Don recalls Burnley as being top of the Football League and notes, with a laugh, that he and his teammates 'thought it might be quite difficult'. Completely undaunted, the team took the game to their higher division hosts, and according to *The Western Daily Press* 'were the more professional, stronger team' as they won 2-1. Indeed the same paper noted that: 'their only regret must be that they didn't defeat Burnley by an even bigger margin. They had a great chance to make the second leg on their main ground a mere formality, but missed so many chances...'

Once again Don was instrumental in the win. On this occasion he didn't score, but he was heavily involved for both of his team's goals. The first of them, late in the first half, came, as the *Evening Advertiser* recorded:

> after Rogers had made a spectacular run and had only been stopped at the expense of an indirect free-kick just outside the home penalty area. Smith's first kick to Rogers had to be retaken because Burnley players were not ten yards from the ball. With everyone on the Burnley side then watching Rogers, Smith chipped the ball over the defence, Noble headed it quickly down to the unmarked Harland who crashed it into the net.

After Burnley had equalised midway through the second half, they must have fancied their chances of taking a first-leg lead. It wasn't to be, as Swindon struck again almost immediately. Don was once more involved, with what *The Advertiser* described as a 'perfect pass' to Peter Noble, who scored what proved to be the winner:

> It was a great result for us obviously, and I think the key was that we genuinely went up there feeling confident. We were on a good run, we knew we could give them a good game, and we thought they would let us play, which always means that you get more of a chance to show what you can do. The problem was that we thought we were through – particularly with our home record.

So two weeks later, on 4 December, Swindon faced the Lancashire side at the County Ground knowing a draw would take them to Wembley. It proved to be a hard game, with the visitors 'often the slightly sharper team in the opening half', having 'proved that they had taken a lesson from the first encounter by playing a far harder brand of football', according to *The Advertiser*. What did that mean, Don? 'They learnt from the first game really, and they didn't give us any room at all. I remember that I hardly got a kick – I was man-marked all the time, and I couldn't get in the game.'

With the half-time score still goalless, Swindon were still on track, but were rocked by two quick goals at the start of the second half, which gave Burnley the lead on aggregate. The home team needed to score now to keep in the tie, and did so within six minutes of Burnley's second, Don's corner being headed in by John Smith. Don felt it was important to score so quickly:

> For John Smith, who was very small, to score with a header was another reason why I felt we were going to win it – he didn't get many with his head! It was critical that we scored straight away because Burnley were showing what a good side they were, and they were well on top at that stage.

2-1 to Burnley at the end of ninety minutes meant that it was extra-time, thirty minutes each way, to decide who would reach Wembley. In the event, neither side could score again, although the unbiased (?) local paper had no doubt as to who should have won:

> Extra-time found both sides looking tired, but it was soon obvious that it was the First Division side who were by far the worse for wear. So much were they overrun during the extra half hour that one could really understand the reason for their jubilation when the final whistle sounded.

It was Swindon's first home defeat for 23 matches in all competitions.

> We were a bit down after the game, because we knew we should have taken our chance in front of our home crowd, and as we've said before, you don't often get more than one chance to beat a better side

– and let's be very clear, Burnley were a better side, in fact probably the best side we faced in the cup run.

Nowadays, we have no second replays; indeed, in what passes for the League Cup, we have no replays at all, with drawn matches decided by penalty shoot-outs. While this may mean less fixture congestion, it does mean that there is no build-up of tension, as ties start to resemble mini seasons in their own right, with each team getting to know each other well, and trying to find a way of exploiting any weakness. However this was 1968 and the semi-final would continue to a replay, and indeed a second, third or fourth replay if needed. The replay would take place on neutral ground, and the venue chosen was The Hawthorns, home of West Bromwich Albion, on 18 December. Despite having apparently missed their chance at The County Ground, Don and his team-mates remained upbeat.

They had every right to be optimistic. After a titanic battle, they eventually won 3-2, after extra time, to get through to Wembley. John Smith scored early on to give Town the lead, and the *Burnley Evening Star* conceded, 'Swindon could have been three up in the first half of normal time'. They protected that lead until the dying seconds when Dave Thomas, later to be a teammate of Don's at Queens Park Rangers scored an equaliser. It was a body blow for Town.

> It was a terrible moment – we thought we were there, and deservedly so, because we'd played very well overall, and being pegged back so close to the final whistle was heartbreaking really...
>
> We showed a lot of bottle – we had a lot of character in the side – and people like Stan and Frank geed us up by shouting; John Smith would encourage us in his quiet way, and generally we were all saying to one another, come on, we can still do this.

Swindon were still adjusting to having been so close to Wembley when Burnley scored again in the first minute of extra time. Now surely the lower division team would fold?

The *Daily Mail* reflected that 'only an astonishing side would recover now, and Swindon were that side'. Town stormed back, missing a couple of good chances before an Arthur Bellamy own goal brought them level just before the end of the first period of extra time. Then, three minutes into the second period of extra time, and with the semi-final now in its 318th minute, Peter Noble scored the goal that took the underdogs to Wembley, still fondly remembered by Don:

> It was a great shot, I do remember that, and once it was in I thought we would win. I don't remember the game personally with any great enthusiasm though – as at Swindon they man-marked me with a full-back called Colin Blant. He followed me everywhere. I used to hate it when people man-marked me – it used to play on my mind the whole game. I'd look round, and see the marker, and think 'not you again'. Teams were clever too, because they always put the quickest players on me. It is very difficult to play against if someone isn't interested in the game, but only interested in stopping you personally from playing.
>
> After the game was very odd. I'm not even sure there was much champagne, if any, in the dressing room afterwards – perhaps they didn't expect us to get through! I do remember getting fish and chips on the way home though to celebrate: very odd when you think about it.

Meanwhile, the question was, how would this cup excitement affect the League form. In previous seasons, good runs had adversely impacted on the day-to-day results in the Third Division, and had cost any chance of promotion.

Our last mention of Swindon's League form was the 5-1 win over Southport on 2 November; in fact between then and the triumph at The Hawthorns, only four League matches were played, with two wins and two defeats. Those games included what Don still remembers as one of the best ever Swindon performances he played in – the 6-2 win at Northampton where all five forwards scored. Then, on the Saturday after a Wembley place was secured, the Town went down to Devon to play Torquay, where they won 1-0 before finishing the year with a 1-0 reverse at Orient on Boxing Day. This left them in fourth place, three points behind leaders Watford but with two games in hand.

ROGERS HITS ONE OF THOSE GOLDEN GOALS

by Steve Richards
(*The Sun*)

Northampton 2   Swindon 6

On a rainy night at Northampton, in front of 6,827 spectators, Swindon's jewel footballer Don Rogers, valued at £100,000 – so they tell us – scored a goal that deserved a setting like Wembley and an audience of 100,000.

Swindon, who, without being ruthless, exposed Northampton's defence, as they became joint leaders of the Third Division again, hope to provide him with the right atmosphere for a repeat in the League Cup final in March if they hold their semi-final lead against Burnley.

Four minutes before the interval, left-winger Rogers collected a clearance from Owen Dawson just beyond the halfway line on a slippery pitch and started a type of spider dribble that you associate only with exceptional players. Rogers had been slipshod in his chance-taking before. This time he made no errors and before putting the ball in the net at his leisure he went around Brian Faulkes, Frank Rankmore and goalkeeper Gordon Morritt.

The goal put Swindon 2-1 ahead after Roberts had headed Northampton into a 16th-minute lead and John Smith had shot the equaliser 15 minutes later.

Northampton had a very promising opening but they did not cash in on goalkeeper Downsborough's trouble in handling the wet ball – except when their goal was helped by his indecisive punch.

When Swindon finally fluttered their wings and unfolded their famous attacking game, they confirmed that they should be imaginative enough to win promotion. If they had taken all their chances they might have created club history!

In the first half I made them leaders on chances and half chances by 10 to 3. After the interval they converted a few more of them and scored the first two of three goals inside three minutes. In the 54th, Roger Smart made it 3-1 after Morritt had obligingly dropped the ball, and in the 55th Don Heath increased the lead following a Rankmore slip.

Northampton came back immediately and Hatton scored their second, created by the clearly roused Rankmore. But in the 74th minute Noble made it 5-2 with a six-yard shot.

Eight minutes from time that man Rogers, now hardly needing to even strain himself by running, danced through the defence to hit his second – and the sixth.

Northampton: Morritt, Faulkes, Fairfax, Townsend, Rankmore, Flowers, Weaver, Kiernan, Hatton, Roberts, Lines. Sub: Brown

Swindon: Downsborough; Dawson, Thomas, Butler, Blick, Harland, Heath, Smart, Smith, Noble, Rogers. Sub: Penman

Now was the real test. The League Cup final, with Arsenal confirmed as their opponents, was still ten weeks away. How would the side react to having such a long period to think about what, for many of them, would be the biggest game of their lives? For Don personally, often the target for some physical punishment, how did he cope with the knowledge that one injury could force him to miss the big day?

I can honestly say that it didn't worry me, mainly because the League games were so crucial. We were going for promotion, and that was far more important to everyone at the club than winning at Wembley. Don't get me wrong, getting to Wembley was great for the town and the directors, but for the players it did take second place to making sure we could play at a higher level.

Money could have been another issue. The weekly magazine *Goal* had a headline in its 11 January issue entitled 'Swindon miss their pay-out'. The article went on to record: 'Because no-one dreamed that Swindon would reach Wembley, nothing about possible extra payments was written into their contracts. Now, because the Football League do not allow contracts to be altered in mid-season, anything extra will depend on the generosity of directors when next season's contracts are considered.'

However, it was not all doom and gloom for the players on the financial front – the article goes on to record that:

> the Third Division side pay their men a crowd bonus of £1 for every 1,000 spectators above 12,000, home or away. This means that the moment they walk out at Wembley, where a 100,000 capacity is surely certain, they'll collect at least £88 per man.

This was better, but not the £2,000 per man that the players of one the teams they had beaten en route to Wembley reportedly stood to earn. Not that it bothered Don and his colleagues: 'We were just so pleased to have got there, and I know I, for one, would have played there for free – money just didn't come into it.'

In the event, the wait seemed to inspire, rather than intimidate. From the start of 1969, the team went on an eleven game run to leave them leading the table. The only sign that Wembley nerves were affecting them was when they lost their last two games, both away, before the big day.

Nowadays, the League Cup final (or its modern-day sponsored equivalent) is played on a Sunday, and is live on TV. There was no such profile for the competition back in the 1960s. The final was played at 3.00 p.m. on a Saturday afternoon, at the same time as all the other football in the country, and yet it was still a huge event, as Don is quick to point out:

> We went up to Wembley to have a look round early on in the week. I'm not sure it helped much, because it was always going to

be very different with 100,000 people there on the Saturday. At
that stage you just want to get on with it – you've had a long wait,
with everyone talking about the game, and you want to get it over.

Everybody, it seemed, wanted to focus on Don. He was the major
star in the Swindon side, and with all due respect to the other ten
players who would start the game for Town, the one who the
general football public were most likely to have heard of. It was not
dissimilar to the situation when the previous Third Division side
had got to the final in 1967 – how many other Queens Park
Rangers players can you name other than Rodney Marsh?

Don wrote an article for *Jimmy Hill's Football Weekly* on the eve
of the final. Reading it, there is none of the brash optimism that
can be found in some of the articles written by today's stars and it is
more a reflection that the game would be tough but that Swindon
at least had a chance.

The experts saw that chance as being slim. Tony Williams,
writing in the same edition of *Jimmy Hills' Football Weekly* that
Don's article appeared in, began his preview with the words
'Arsenal must win!' although he acknowledged Don as a 'brilliant
winger', who was likely to receive special attention from legendary
Arsenal hard man, Peter Storey. Peter Barnard, writing in the
League Cup final edition of *Goal* headlined his piece 'It must be
Arsenal', although again he acknowledged that Don was a 'poten-
tial matchwinner'.

The stars interviewed for their views, also for *Goal*, selected Don
for special praise as well, although were also keen to acknowledge
the team ethic, and the 'fine defence'. Bobby Charlton remarked
that 'Swindon have very good individual players like winger Don
Rogers, and they play with a great deal of method, discipline and
tight organisation'. Former Swindon winger Mike Summerbee
remarked 'in Don Rogers they have a bloke who could win the
League Cup for them'.

John Trollope recalls: 'Don was obviously our star player and
nobody ever resented him getting the headlines. We accepted that

he would change games. We had a really good side with lots of good players, but Don was the icing on the cake – and every great side needs players who can do something special.'

Rod Thomas agrees: 'Don was very popular with the lads, because although he was what you would call our glamour player, there was never any edge or side to him. He was, and still is, a really genuine bloke, who is extremely modest. We used to tease him of course, because we said he came off with clean shorts every week, but he could do something in ten minutes of brilliance that would change a game completely.'

Nobody really gave the Third Division side a chance. True, the Arsenal side of 1969 were nowhere near as strong, relatively speaking, as their modern-day equivalents, but this was still a good team, and was the nucleus of the side that would go on to win the 'Double' (League Championship and FA Cup) in 1971. What is more, most of the side had recent experience of playing at Wembley, as Arsenal had contested the previous season's League Cup final, losing 1-0 to Leeds. They were widely expected to put that defeat behind them, not that Don and his teammates were bothered that people were writing them off.

> It really helped us being the underdogs, because there was no pressure on us. I know that's what most lower division sides would say, but it was definitely true for us. We really fancied our chances though – we knew what we could do, and we certainly weren't going there to lose.

The team travelled down to their Wembley hotel on the Friday; for Don and his teammates it was then a case of waiting:

> I remember us going for a walk on the Friday night, and although it took me a while to get off to sleep, I had a good night. Then it was up for breakfast about nine o'clock – scrambled eggs, as usual after an overnight stay – before we went out for another walk. Then we watched the television – again like we usually did on

away trips, except of course this time we were on all the lunchtime football shows – and then it was lunch – steak, toast and tea – before we set off for Wembley. We were all ready to go by then. When we got close to the stadium it was unbelievable. All the Swindon fans cheering us and waving to us; the atmosphere was incredible. I can't imagine what it must have been like for an FA Cup final – our final was good enough!

There was a lot of controversy about the pitch. The Horse of the Year Show had recently been staged at Wembley, and the pitch was, shall we say, just a little muddy… Don though wasn't worried:

When you play football, you've got to play on whatever surface you are given to play on. You just get on and play. They said the surface at Wembley suited us, and I think it probably did – it was just like the County Ground. I used to say that from September to March I played my home games on mud! I still cannot believe how bad some of the pitches were we played on: nowadays the games would never take place. They were so desperate to play the games in those days they used to use a lot of sand on the pitches, which of course made things worse. I've played in games, particularly at Swindon, where the ball would barely roll two yards. So, whilst the surface for the League Cup final wasn't very good, this was less unusual than it would be now.

It was to be Don's finest hour, yet those famous images of him scoring in the Wembley mud so nearly didn't happen. That was because his side came within four minutes of winning the game in normal time through Roger Smart's goal in the first half. Poor Roger Smart; I suspect that, though delighted that his side won, he felt a little like Martin Peters after the 1966 World Cup final in that he was denied the glory of being the matchwinner, instead seeing his thunder stolen by a teammate who scored twice in extra time. It was Bobby Gould who scored the Arsenal equaliser to take it into the added period, and, like the equaliser England conceded in extra injury time in 1966, it came desperately close to the end of the game. Did Don think the game was up?

> We were thinking we've done it – we're there, and then Bobby Gould scored the goal, and that really knocked us down. I lost the ball for the goal as well. If you see the film, I've lost it in their half. I was a bit unlucky because I knocked it a bit too far, otherwise I would have been in, so it was partly my fault that the goal went in.

Don readily acknowledges that without the Arsenal goal, the final would have been remembered very differently:

> I've always said that there is a very fine line between being a hero and being a nobody – had it been 1-0 everyone would have remembered more about Peter Downsborough, because he played really well that day. He stopped everything that came at him, they could have scored six or seven really.

So, as against Burnley in the semi-final, the team had conceded a late goal. What was said as the players regrouped before the extra thirty minutes?

> We still fancied our chances, partly because we knew that they had been suffering from a flu bug during the previous week and there-fore might be more tired than us, because we all still felt we had full tanks. If you look at the video, then we had as much of the game as them in extra time: it was probably our best spell.

And so to extra time, where Don scored the two goals that made him a national star. The *Sunday Express* described his first:

> Then another corner, Penman, who had come on as a substitute for Smith 12 minutes before the end of full-time, hooked at the ball with his back to goal and it fell at the feet of Noble. He was blocked but the ball screwed to Rogers. With the coolness of a Puskas or Di

Stefano, Rogers took the ball with his right foot, beat one man on a sixpence and smashed it in with his left from close range.

What does Don remember of the goal? 'The goal was probably a lot harder than it looked. Pete Noble had a swing at the ball, and it came to me, so I dragged it with my right foot, and put it in the net first time with my left foot. The key was that I did it all so quickly, and that's why it went in.'

And then came the goal for which Don is best remembered, described like this by our old friend the *Evening Advertiser*:

> Nothing could stop Swindon now and they clinched the match completely with a further goal in the second extra-time period. Butler checked a left-wing run by Ure and slid a quick pass to Smart. The inside-right waited for a moment, steadied himself, and then pushed the ball into the path of Rogers, who was just inside the Swindon half. With the Arsenal defenders never looking like catching him, the outside-left raced completely clear, and took the ball right up to the advancing Wilson. As the goalkeeper dived, Rogers then whipped it past him on the outside and placed his shot accurately into the net.

Don can recall the goal, one of the most oft-replayed moments in the club's history, with enormous clarity:

> When Roger put me through, I remember thinking, hang on, I'm in here. Then I thought, I'm going to have to go round Bob Wilson, because I'm so far out, he's going to come and meet me in a minute, and I knew nobody else was going to catch me and that it was just me and the 'keeper. I still think I was a bit lucky, because when I went past him it was on a nice flat part of the pitch, so the ball didn't bobble, which it could have done, given how bad the pitch was. If you dream of how to finish the game off, that would have been it – run half the length of the field, round the 'keeper, and knock it into the net.

The goalkeeper he beat to score his goals, Bob Wilson, said after the game: 'He took his second goal brilliantly. As I came out it was just him and me, but he dummied me brilliantly before cracking the ball home from a really acute angle.'

John Trollope remembers the goals well, as you'd expect:

Don's first goal was a bit of a scramble – he shifted the ball out from under his feet, like he was so good at doing – and then of course the second goal was his run from 50 yards: he just dipped his shoulder and put the ball in the net. I knew then we had won. Clearly Don was the star, but don't forget Peter Downsborough. If it wasn't for him in the first half, we wouldn't have been in the game.

Frank Burrows is keen to dwell on Don's overall performance:

It wasn't just the goals. From the second half onwards Don and Don Heath, the two wingers, terrorised them. Yes, of course he scored two great goals, but his contribution was much, much more than that – his movement, his control, his passing. There were always some rumours outside of the club about his fitness, but if you look at the video, he was absolutely flying in extra-time, so no problems on that score.

The club recently released a video of the full game. It was the first time I had ever seen all 120 minutes. One is struck by just how bad the pitch was, but also by the way Don made light of it, particularly to score his goals. It was a team effort and the whole side will look back with pride on their performances, but it wasn't just the goals, as Frank Burrows says, that meant Don made many of the headlines.

Now, thirty-five years on, what can Don remember about the day, and about the celebrations?

I suppose there are three or four memories of the day that have stuck with me. The first was in the bath after the game at Wembley – about ten of us in the big communal bath drinking champagne. I suppose that was as good as it could get really. The next memory is the fact that we struggled to get back to the hotel for the meal and we had virtually no time to change. We just ran upstairs and came back down to dinner, in about five minutes flat. Bob Monkhouse was the comedian at the celebration, and he was absolutely brilliant. He'd really done his homework, so he spoke about local areas like Purton, mentioned most of the players' names; I think he felt very lucky to be at the winners' event, because he must have thought he would have been with the runners-up. Then the bar closed really early – about one o'clock in the morning – which was a shame because I think we would have been happy to have stayed up all night.

ROGERS... AND OUT!
Swindon genius rubs Arsenal in the mud
by Maurice Smith

Arsenal 1 Swindon 3

The mudstains on the Arsenal shirts told the tale of the day when eleven players from the humble Third Division became giants. For Arsenal were not merely beaten by these men of Swindon – they were demoralised, run into the ground, made so often to look second-class. This was a triumph of adventure. Arsenal set out to play it defensively with a stolid, unambitious 4-3-3 formation. That against a side two grades below them – on paper!

Swindon, on the other hand, went for 4-2-4. And made it pay by dominating the midfield. I say by doing that Swindon have not only done themselves but the whole of football the good turn of the season – perhaps for many seasons to come. For surely this was the death knell of mere rugged defence.

Salute them all, these heroes from the West. But I demand an extra-special ovation for the man who took Wembley by storm... who made this cup final in the mud his own triumph. The name: DON ROGERS.

Rogers was the genius who had international defenders like Ure, McNab and McLintock looking over their shoulders every time he had the ball. Rogers never wasted a ball, looked always before he made his move – and always had Arsenal wondering where and how he was going to strike next. It was Rogers who scored the two extra-time goals, both deliberate, immaculate one-man strikes, after Arsenal had managed to pull the game out of the fire with an equaliser six minutes from the end.

His second goal came from a great weaving run that ended in his side-stepping the goalkeeper and bulging the net with a Bobby Charlton-style drive. That seemed to sum it all up. It was Rogers the master and Arsenal the mastered.

Arsenal's Jon Samuels summed it up too, when after firing in a tremendous shot in the dying moments of the original 90 minutes, he saw 'keeper Downsborough respond with an even greater save. Samuels sank to the ground and beat the Wembley ground with his fists in sheer frustration. And sheer frustration represented the end of so much of this Arsenal effort.

Swindon wouldn't get a look in, they'd told us. But it was Swindon, right from the start, fighting for every ball, calling the tune. When Smart put them ahead it was no more than they deserved. And this goal high-lighted Arsenal's early attitude.

Ure was so casual in turning the ball back to his advancing goalkeeper, Wilson. All they managed to do was to set up the easiest of chances for Smart. And all the credit for making the goal in the first place belonged to that man Rogers. Calmly he had run fifty yards with the ball, cutting through the Arsenal defence as though it had ceased to exist.

But if Arsenal were casual early on, any sign of casualness left them. They realised just what they had to beat in these men of the West. And hard though they fought, they were never equal to the task. When they were on target, goalkeeper Downsborough was there to send them back.

Ironically, it was Downsborough's mistake that led to Gould giving Arsenal their extended chance six minutes from the end. He came out too late, fumbled as Gould shot, and gave the Arsenal man a second chance to nod that ill-deserved equaliser.

Arsenal – again a sign of desperation – had replaced successful defender Simpson with extra striker Graham. And Swindon's midfield director Smith came off for Penman.

The question as they went into extra-time was whether Swindon could last on this stamina-sapping pitch on which all of them were appearing for the first time.

Last? They hardly let Arsenal have a single kick in that thirty minutes of extra time. And there could have been a fourth to add to their total. A drive from Trollope was sailing into the Arsenal net when it struck the referee and all Swindon got was a corner.

In a match in which police several times had to remove turbulent Arsenal fans, only one player got into any trouble when Swindon's Heath had his name taken for kicking the ball away in disgust when he thought a foul was awarded the wrong way.

Swindon: Downsborough 8; Thomas 8, Burrows 8, Harland 8, Trollope 7; Butler 8, Smith (withdrawn) 8: Heath 6, Smart 7, Noble 7, ★ROGERS 9. Sub: Penman 7

Arsenal: Wilson 7; Storey 7, Ure 7, Simpson (withdrawn) 7; Court 7, ★SAMUELS 8, McLintock 6; Radford 7, Gould 7, Armstrong 7. Sub: Graham 6

So Swindon had won, and deservedly so. Inevitably the headlines were all about Don: '100,000 hail hero Rogers', 'It's Rogers and out for Arsenal' (they were just as bad at headline writing back then as they are today). Don was now, without doubt, a major star. Wiltshire's best-kept secret was out:

It had a major impact on the rest of my life, not so much my career, because of course I stayed at Swindon, although I know clubs were trying to buy me – Manchester City, and one or two of the London clubs. But in terms of my life, it was a major event, because even now when I'm on holiday, people will come up to me and say – 'Ah Don Rogers, Wembley against Arsenal, we remember you.'

John Trollope recalls: 'It's a blur to be honest – the first time we had ever been there and we certainly didn't expect to go there and go up those steps to get the cup. My main memory is on the Sunday coming back. I've never seen so many people, it seemed like all of Swindon was out to cheer.'

Don agrees with his friend's recollections:

> I came back separately in a limo on the Sunday, because I did an interview at the ITV studios first while everyone else went back on the bus. We then had lunch at The Goddard Arms. Swindon was unbelievable – there were people everywhere. I don't think there was anybody indoors at all. It really united the town – I believe football can do that, and it certainly did so for Swindon that year.

One final memory for Don, a very personal one: 'Everyone was surprised because on the video of the game, you can see me swear with the camera right on my face, and nobody had ever heard me swear before. So I got some stick for that from the lads, with everyone drawing attention to it…'

I think that without the events of thirty-five years ago at Wembley, it is unlikely that you would be reading this book. Don would still be fondly remembered of course, and would still go down as one of the great wingers, but he would be a local, rather than a national, name. Indeed, perhaps he owes a lot to Bobby Gould…

Wembley was then the cue for more national acclaim for Don. Not only did all the newspapers focus on him, but the football magazines also took the opportunity to have their say. Bernard Bale, writing in *Goal* asked 'if Don Rogers was rated at £100,000 before the Wembley showpiece, then what price now?' George Best, writing in *Jimmy Hill's Football Weekly* said:

Don Rogers? Good player, isn't he? We played against him and Swindon in the youth cup some years back and he looked a very good player, even then. He's got pretty well all the talents obviously, but he's just been a bit doubtful away from home on the few occasions I've seen him in action.

Dodgy away from home... Mike Summerbee mentioned something similar in his preview of the final saying 'He (Don) is a better player at home than away'. The same could be said of the whole Swindon team around this era, as we have seen and we will return to this subject later.

Perhaps unsurprisingly, the team lost the first League game after Wembley, 2-1 at Plymouth on the following Saturday, the memory of which brings a wry smile to Don's lips – 'I'm not surprised. The celebrations seemed to go on for two weeks!' This meant that, with eleven games to go, promotion was by no means assured. However, they only lost one of those games, a 1-0 home defeat to Watford on 29 March, in front of nearly 29,000. It was a defeat which ultimately cost them the Third Division Championship.

We would have won the Championship comfortably if we'd beaten Watford. The atmosphere was tremendous and there were so many people locked out – there must have been well over 30,000 trying to get into the ground. I also remember the away game at Watford. That was the only time I got caught badly: their fullback came straight across me, very deliberately, and kicked me when I was clean though. It really hurt, I can tell you. He would have been sent off now of course.

Frank Burrows remembers a game towards the end of the season at Fellows Park, Walsall, which Swindon won 2-0, Don scoring both goals:

Don scored some incredible goals the season we did the League Cup and promotion double. We played at Walsall, and it was a terrible day – chucking it down – an awful day for football. They were battering us. Their centre forward, George Kirby, was kicking lumps out of Stan Harland and me. Anyway, we got one ball out of defence and Willie Penman played the ball through to Don, who went clean through like a rocket, beat the centre half and the covering defender and scored. Then it was backs to the wall again. They were playing down the slope towards the River End, battering us again. Then, the same story, either Willie, or Joe Butler, both of whom were great passers, put the ball through and Don went through again and scored to make it 2-0.

We played in all-white, and as we walked off the pitch, covered in mud, we saw Don walking off with just a couple of flecks of mud on his shorts – you could still the crease on his shorts. Rod Thomas turned to me and said 'Look at him – we're covered in mud, he's almost clean, and he's the one who's scored the goals!' But that's what Don gave us, he could make and score goals out of nothing – he was a superb finisher.

Promotion was eventually secured at Rotherham on 2 May, where a late goal by Chris Jones, at the club where manager Danny Williams had made his name, secured the second leg of Swindon's very own 'double'.

I didn't know we'd scored in the last minute up there, but I do remember that there weren't really that many celebrations – perhaps because we still had one game to go at home, and I think we all thought we would be going up anyway. I know there wasn't much champagne, if any, in the dressing room, which struck me as a bit odd.

It had been a fantastic season. Why had the club done so well?

The real secret was that the key fourteen or fifteen players all got on so well together, which believe me is most unusual in a dressing room. We were all good friends and just got on with our jobs. I used to get a lot of headlines of course, due to my goals, which could have annoyed others, because they were doing their jobs really well, but nobody got upset – there was just a lot of mickey-taking! I used to get a bit worried by it to be honest, but I think they knew I was embarrassed, which probably helped, so nobody got jealous. Everyone knew we all appreciated one another and we all knew what our roles were.

When I met Frank Burrows, I asked him the same question. The defender, now a long-standing manager and coach, for ten minutes, with the aid of a sheet of paper, he gave the tactical answer to that question.

We had a great system – way before people talked at length about 4-4-2 and 4-5-1 and all that kind of stuff. Peter Noble was our centre forward, with John Smith, who was a great passer of the ball but couldn't run, operating in the space just behind him. Our second striker was Don, who played out on the left wing, in theory. Don Heath played on the right wing, Roger Smart inside him, and Joe Butler inside Don. Joe just sat in the space to cover for Don, and also for John Trollope who was always overlapping.

Where we caused everyone problems was that we played with two strikers, but the second one was Donald. We were playing a flexible system, without knowing it at the time. What it meant was that one centre half would take Peter Noble, and then the other centre half had nobody to mark, because they didn't want to go out on the wing and mark Don, and they didn't want to go and mark John Smith either As soon as Don's full-back came forward, Don was all by himself out on the wing, and people like Roger Smart, John Smith and Joe Butler were such good passers of the ball that they could always get the ball out to him. Once he had the ball he had lots of space to work in, and away he would go. It was a great system for us; it was based on the workrate of some of our midfield players like Joe, Don Heath and Roger who did the work of two people each, and it meant we could play to our strength, which was Don Rogers – it freed him up to stay on the halfway line. Later on, teams started to stop their right-back coming forward at all, to make sure he stayed back to mark Don.

I'm not sure we all realised what we were doing at the time – it was only after I took all my coaching badges I could tell you how we played. In tight matches we did play 4-5-1. Don did come back, although it was like pulling teeth! Usually though, Don didn't come back at all, he just mooched on the halfway line, and I love him for it, because he got me a lot of win bonuses!

Don was, inevitably, at the heart of the season's success with 29 League and cup goals. This time those goals had brought a huge reward. It was back to the Second Division.

It was definitely the best season of my career, no doubt about it – both in terms of what we achieved and also because it was such a good team to play in, with that atmosphere. The manager had a lot to do with it too: he was always happy, and it gets through to the players. We always used to laugh at his team talks as well – I remember he had us in stitches when he called Dick Krzywicki, the Huddersfield full-back Krzy Wizzy Wicky – we all loved that. He used to say things to me like 'The full-back can't run Don – you'll be all right', when he was like a greyhound! A great guy though Danny, and he was helped by the fact that it was such a strong dressing room; it was a great time to be playing for the club.

Back in the Second

Don and his teammates returned for pre-season training in good heart, believing that they had a good chance of making a real impact on the Second Division. The side that had won the League Cup had been kept together, although there was one major addition to the squad, striker Arthur Horsfield from Middlesbrough. Don recalls:

> We were all on a high from the previous season and, I think, although we didn't really talk about it, we all thought that we had a good chance of going straight through to the First Division. We knew we were a good side, and we'd stayed together, and so there was a great sense of belief amongst the players.

However, as Swindon prepared for the beginning of the season, they were rocked by a high-profile departure; not one of the players, but the manager. After four seasons in charge, Danny Williams decided to take up the managerial reigns at First Division Sheffield Wednesday, and returned to his native Yorkshire. Don, along with the rest of the squad, was surprised:

> All of sudden he'd gone – I think we found out through the radio. It was a big shock to us all. Looking back though I can see that he

must have thought it was a dream move for him, going back home to his roots, to a bigger club, with a great ground – one of the best in England. There were no hard feelings though, we just all told him what we'd done for him to help him land a job like that!

Williams' replacement was Fred Ford, then manager at Bristol Rovers, and a man known to most of the squad, having spent a spell as chief coach at the County Ground in the 1967/68 season.

We all knew Fred of course, and his appointment happened very quickly so there was no unrest amongst the players. I think we were all happy with him as our new manager – he was well liked and respected. He was a big fellow, mind, with a temper to match. I can give you an example of that: it must have been after a Saturday when we lost – we were training on the Monday morning, just jogging around the County Ground – about twenty or thirty of us in twos, having a good chat. We got to the top of the ground, the Stratton Bank End, and Fred Ford shouted at the top of his voice 'Stop!' Then he came over and said 'if you lot don't stop yakking, I'll take everyone of you behind the stands and give you a good hiding.' As you can imagine, the talking stopped!

Don has another humorous anecdote about a man whom he was clearly very fond of. Although Fred Ford is sadly not with us to confirm that the feeling is mutual, one suspects it was – remember it was Ford who was beaten by Bert Head to Don's signature back in the early 1960s.

Fred had part of one of his fingers missing, and he used to get some real stick behind his back for that. In the dressing room he used to say, 'I want four in the wall', but of course because he only had half of one of his fingers, it looked like three in the wall, and people like Rod Thomas and Pete Noble would be behind him holding up three fingers – all good natured but great fun. You had to keep a straight face because Fred would have gone mad if he had found out. Thommo and Pete Downsborough used to do that in the game as well: hold up three fingers for a four-man wall. It was one of our in-jokes.

I remember his first conversation with me; it was at a time when I was negotiating a new contract, and he pulled me over away from the other players and said 'Don, about this new contract – I don't want to have anything to do with it. You sort it out with the chairman', and he was as good as his word.

Surely Don was in a great negotiating position for that new contract given his heroics the previous season?

I can honestly say that I didn't think like that. I was happy at Swindon, both on and off the field; I was enjoying my life, and the team was being successful. What more do you want? I wouldn't have negotiated hard like they do nowadays – money isn't everything, as long as you've got enough.

This was to be, until the days of Lou Macari, Ossie Ardiles and Glenn Hoddle, Swindon's most successful season ever. The team took a little time to settle into the higher division, with just three wins in their first twelve matches, but then lost only two of the next twenty-five to put themselves right into the thick of another promotion battle. It was a remarkable run, particularly when one considers the fact that they were playing at a higher level. Don says the start was no bad thing:

We did find it a little harder to start with. There were some good teams in that league and they were better, week in week out, than we had been used to, and it wasn't as rosy as we thought it was going to be to start with, which was probably a good thing because it got us focused.

The side was very settled, which always helps. Ten players played more than thirty-five games, including Don, although he missed six games after picking up an injury against Hull in October. The side, when everybody was fit, picked itself: Peter Downsborough in goal, Rod Thomas and John Trollope as the full-backs with centre halves Frank Burrows and Stan Harland completing the defence. The regular midfielders were Don, Roger Smart and Joe Butler, with the fourth member one of Don Heath or John Smith. Up front it was Peter Noble and Arthur Horsfield.

> The side being settled was obviously key – we all knew each other's game and how we wanted to play. It was slightly different from the previous season in that Arthur had come in and we therefore played 4-4-2 rather than a more fluid formation with just Pete Noble up front.

There is no doubt that the Second Division was harder. In each of the previous seasons, the team had scored more than 70 League goals; this year they would score 57. For Don personally, having scored 24, 25 and 22 League goals in the last three years, this year would see a fall off in League goals to 9. He comments: 'I think part of this was down to how we played, with two up front. There was less space for me to come into, running inside the full-back. I reverted more to being a creator that year, my job was to go on the outside of the full-back not the inside.'

After a 1-0 defeat at Norwich on Good Friday, 30 March, Swindon had five games to play. The first of these was the home game against Birmingham the next day, which was won 4-1. Don scored twice, one of them from the penalty spot. They were now right in the midst of the promotion race, being in fourth place, but with games in hand on third-placed Cardiff City. 'We thought we were going up, we really did. We were unstoppable at home, and confidence was very high. We just brushed Birmingham aside, and they were by no means a bad side.'

The first of the four games was at the inhospitable venue of The Den, home of Millwall, only a mid-table side, but one with a great home record. Despite another Don goal, the team lost 3-1, which meant that the game against Blackpool at the County Ground would be critical – with the visitors lying in second place.

In front of 28,500 the home side got off to a great start, with Arthur Horsfield scoring in the first minute, but Blackpool equalised to severely dent Swindon's promotion hopes. Those hopes were all but extinguished when they lost 3-0 at home to Middlesbrough the following week, their first home defeat of the season. Looking back, Don says:

> Blackpool were a very good side. They had a lot of very good players – the lad who got their goal, Micky Burns, especially. We should have won though, we got a great start, and had all the pressure, but couldn't finish them off. Then against Middlesbrough, we were well beaten – no complaints, they deserved to win, and we didn't play very well.

The side eventually finished in fifth place, three points behind second-placed Blackpool. They had been very close to securing top-flight football. Had they been able to win more than just four away games, they probably would have done so.

Often, newly-promoted clubs can do very well in a higher division. They have a level of momentum, and confidence, that comes from having been promoted, and they also have the advantage of the 'surprise factor'. With the benefit of hindsight, does Don feel that the best chance of promotion went when the team just missed out in that first season?

> That was our best chance to go up. We were never going to get a team like that again, especially one that had been brought together so cheaply. When you look back on it, all the players were worth far more after a few years at Swindon than when they had signed, and it was an exceptional team for a town like Swindon. I think that had we gone up we would have done well against the better sides we played – we'd have got a couple of new players, and

the nucleus of the team was good enough to play in the top flight. It was a real family club as well; that always helped us; I always used to reckon that I knew at least 15,000 of the people who went to the home games personally – I'd met them somehow, at my shop, or I'd presented them with something. Don't underestimate how valuable that was – a real sense of community, both on and off the pitch.

John Trollope agrees: 'Looking back, we had a great chance of going straight through and were disappointed that we didn't. We were good enough, there's no doubt about it – four of that side played in the top division, and others could have done so.'

Frank Burrows, with the benefit of managerial experience, has a clear view:

1968/69 and 1969/70 were the best two years of my football life, no question about it. We all mixed well, and got on with each other, which of course was helped by the fact that we were winning. We should have gone up that season, and I think the reason we didn't was that we didn't strengthen the side. We needed people in to freshen us up, and to provide a challenge to those who were there – give them more pressure to achieve. Had we done that I think we would have gone up.

Once more there was also a great cup run to savour. This wasn't in the League Cup, where, as holders, they lost at Oxford (of all places) in the third round, but in the FA Cup, where they had their best run since 1912. Town scored eleven goals in three matches to reach the sixth round: a 4-0 win at Blackburn was followed by comfortable home wins over Chester and Scunthorpe, the latter of whom included a young Kevin Keegan in their side, a name Don could have played with...

There's a story about Keegan. After we played them, some of our directors went to watch him at Scunthorpe with a view to signing him, only to decide that he was too small – perhaps not the best decision!'

Frank Burrows had been with Kevin Keegan at Scunthorpe, and he confirms the story: 'Fred Ford called me into the office and asked me about Kevin, and I know they were very interested in him. However, they didn't pursue it, which I felt at the time was a mistake.

The sixth round draw gave them a home tie with Don Revie's Leeds United, then the strongest team in the country. Don and his team mates were delighted:

> They were definitely the best side in the competition, no doubt about it. At the time, we were all delighted, because you want to play against the best teams. I know it sounds funny now, but we did think we could beat them. We were such a good side at home, and thought we had a chance of catching them unaware given how tight the ground was.

Once again, the media descended on Wiltshire. There was a genuine possibility of an upset – although this would have been the equivalent of the team defeating the modern-day Arsenal or Manchester United.

Goal magazine ran a preview under the heading of 'Rogers faces his greatest test', and focused on his England ambitions:

> Just as Londoners, particularly Chelsea fans, are convinced that Peter Osgood should be in Sir Alf Ramsay's England squad for Mexico, so one regularly hears the chant at Swindon, 'Rogers for England'. Don Rogers, hero of the County Ground, has won under-23 honours for his country. But generally he has not seemed to fit into the England team-manager's line of thinking, despite a succession of top-line performances during Swindon's climb in the last two years. Now the sixth round of the FA Cup offers Rogers the finest ever chance to stake his claim for an England place, for there can be no

tougher test than to play against Leeds United, the Football League champions, and favourites to win the European Cup.

The article goes on to pay tribute to Don's 'deceptive pace, amazing control and superb shot in both feet' and also quotes Maurice Lindley, the Leeds assistant manager, as saying that Swindon were 'the best footballing side in the Second Division that I have seen... I rate them as good, very good.'

The game itself was an anticlimax. Allan Clarke scored twice for the visitors in the first half and Swindon never looked like coming back. They weren't helped by the fact that their star player was under the weather, and got out of his sick bed to play.

> They were much better than us, and won the game easily. They were the best side I ever played against – quality everywhere, all internationals. From my point of view, I had a very tough after-noon against Paul Reaney, who marked me out of the game. I remember saying to him at half-time as we were coming off – are you coming in our dressing room as well – I'd had enough by then. As I've said before, it's very difficult if you are man-marked by someone who only focuses on you and not the game. The only chance you've got is if you are quicker than your marker, but Reaney was very quick.

There was to be some cup success this season, however, albeit in a somewhat controversial fashion. Swindon, as League Cup winners the previous season, should have entered the Fairs Cup (now the UEFA Cup) for 1969/70, but, like Queens Park Rangers before them, were not allowed to compete, as they were a Third Division side – although, as Don says, they knew the rules:

> We knew we wouldn't be allowed to compete because QPR had the same problem a couple of years earlier. It was unfair though. There was no reason why they shouldn't have allowed us to play – after all we had won the cup fair and square against a First Division

side. It was a shame; I would have loved to have tried my luck in Europe, and as we showed in the competitions we were allowed to play in, we would have done well.

As a consolation, a hastily arranged tournament, the Anglo-Italian Cup Winners' Cup, was set up. It sounds like something out of a Jasper Carrott sketch, but in fact it was played between Swindon and the Italian Cup winners, AS Roma, over two legs. The first leg was played in Italy on 27 August 1969, and in front of 40,000 spectators, Swindon were beaten by 2-1. They turned that round comfortably enough in the second leg though, winning 4-0 on 3 September, with Don's goal being somewhat overshadowed by an Arthur Horsfield hat-trick. A crowd of just 15,000 (at a time when average home League gates were significantly higher) indicated that the Swindon public were perhaps not convinced by the competition.

It was a great experience playing in Rome, and we played very well indeed, which made it better. We were unlucky to lose there. We made up for it in the home leg – we absolutely hammered them at the County Ground, one of our best performances of the season, if not of my time at Swindon. It was like playing in a real European competition with the home and away leg – good for the players, good for the club.

At the end of the season there was another Anglo-Italian competition to take part in: the Anglo-Italian Cup. This competition achieved real notoriety when it was reintroduced in the mid-1990s, but in its first incarnation it was taken seriously enough. The rules were complex though; I can do no better than quote them directly from Paul Plowman's excellent statistical record of the club *Swindon Town: To Wembley and Beyond*:

Contested by six Football League clubs and six Italian League clubs. Two clubs from each league formed into groups. Each Football League club played twice against the two Italian clubs in its group, once in England and once in Italy. Bonus points were awarded for each goal scored. The highest-placed club from England and Italy respectively contested for a gold cup, sponsored by Esso Petroleum.

The matches were played over May, and Swindon found themselves drawn with the Italian clubs SS Napoli and Juventus.

The first game saw Juventus at the County Ground. This sounds bizarre now, and even then Juventus were one of the top Italian clubs (the following year they would lose to Leeds in the final of the old Fairs Cup). However, they were well beaten in Wiltshire on 2 May, losing 4-0. Next up were Napoli, also at the County Ground, a week later and this time Swindon were beaten by 2-1 to leave their qualification very much in the balance.

On 16 May, Town were in Italy to play Juventus. Remarkably, they won 1-0 in Turin, thanks to Peter Noble's goal. They now had a chance of going through, aided by the results of the other English teams, and by the bonus points from the win over Juventus.

They were incredible results. Just imagine it now, Swindon Town beating Juventus, home and away, particularly to win in Italy. I think we were a very strange team for those Italian teams to play against because we were prepared to run at them at pace, and they just weren't used to it. They couldn't cope with it.

To get through they would need to win in Naples against Napoli. Win it they did, 1-0, with Don scoring the goal in front of 30,000.

In the final, they would play Napoli again. Despite their defeat by Town, the Southern Italian side had finished the best-placed of the Italian sides competing. The final would be in the same Naples stadium where Swindon had just won, only five days previously.

We were in Italy for ten days and it was a great trip. We didn't train at all – we laid on the beach in the morning and then played tennis in the afternoon. In fact we had a big tournament, organised by Fred, we all had to go and sit on the sidelines and cheer on whoever was playing. In the evening we went out for a drink at a local bar; nothing silly, but Fred was happy about it – it was relaxation really, and he knew we'd look after ourselves – the odd run up and down the beach, or at least the keener ones did, I'm not sure that I did!

The funny thing on that trip was when Fred got ill. We got a really big lecture from him about not drinking the tap water, and we were all fine… but Fred ended up very sick, because he didn't follow his own advice. We found it very funny – not that we showed that to Fred's face of course!

In the event, the final was very one-sided. Two goals by Peter Noble and one by Arthur Horsfield gave Swindon a comfortable win. Even though the Italian fans rioted before the end of the game, and the match was never finished, the result was allowed to stand. As Don says 'We were so far ahead the referee just said to us – you've won, now let's get off the pitch!'

John Trollope remembers the final only too well: 'I suddenly realised that Don was on the other side of the pitch, and wondered why. Then a lump of concrete came on to the pitch from the stand and I soon knew – all the rioting was on our side.'

Don grins when I tell him his full-back's recollection: 'John is absolutely right. Something came over my head, and I looked down and realised it was a piece of rock. Then there was more, and the rocks were getting bigger, so I moved five yards from the touchline, then ten yards, and in the end I decided that's it, I'm going on the other side!'

Even though the focus of the football world was more on the World Cup in Mexico, the win still brought more national coverage. Bobby Charlton, writing in *Goal* congratulated Swindon on their victory and noted that 'I'll bet Swindon are now a better side for the Italian experience they wouldn't otherwise have received' and Stuart Shaw, writing in *Soccer Star*, noted 'the Englishmen thoroughly outplayed Napoli'.

On a different note, Trollope sees these matches of further evidence of Don's quality:

Against those Italian sides, Don showed what a really good player he was. The Italians simply weren't used to it with all their defensive play and games ending 1-0. Don did the same as he did in England – he ran at players, and I could have seen him being a real hero in Italian football.

Don himself agrees:

The Italians just weren't used to players like me. I would have loved to have played in Italy but it never happened. I don't know if anyone actually came in for me. I know there were lots of rumours at that time. The one thing that I don't think is generally well known is that one of the American clubs tried to sign me about then, but nothing came of it – not sure I would have fancied that, but it was an interesting thought.

It had been another great season. Two cups, a place in the last eight of the FA Cup, and the club's highest-ever League position. Life seemed bright, both for the club and their star winger.

The summer of 1970 was a time to take stock. England were, unsuccessfully, defending the World Cup in Mexico. Don had now played seven full seasons of League football, and well over 300 games in League and cup, yet he was only twenty-five. How did he see his career in that summer?

I was delighted with how things had gone over the past two years – lots of success, playing with my mates, at a club that I loved. Moving on was the last thing on my mind. I was enjoying it too much, and we all thought that we would have another good season the next time round.

John Trollope was delighted that Don had been such a success: 'Don had proved that at whatever level he played he could score goals and create chances. I think he benefited from the step up. The standard was better and teams tried to play more football and were less likely to try and kick you.'

Frank Burrows would describe playing with Don at that time as a privilege:

> I was lucky, and that team was lucky in that it had such a gifted player as Don Rogers. We were fortunate in that he liked Swindon – the fans, the town and the club, and of course he was playing in a winning team and scoring goals. He was really gifted and had balance, pace, good feet, power – people forget that Don wasn't much under six feet tall. He had real moments of greatness. Had he been playing today, he would have played in the First Division sooner – freedom of contract and all that.

Rod Thomas was keen that Don's wider abilities as a footballer be remembered:

> Of course people will remember Don for his ability to go past players, and also for his ability to beat the goalkeeper one-on-one, but he also had an outstanding football brain. He regularly used to put John Trollope in down the left wing, and John didn't need to check his run – the ball just arrived at his feet.

Yet with hindsight, the decision to stay at Swindon may have been the wrong one, at least from a professional sense. If there was a time to go then this was it. Don was in his prime, clubs were keen to sign him, and although we didn't know it at the time, Swindon would struggle to have the same impact as a side that they had achieved in their first season in the Second Division. Had he moved then, he would have had two extra years in the First Division, and the impact on his career might have been huge.

The 1970/71 season proved to be an enormous disappointment. Once more the problem was predominantly in the away form. Only three matches were won, and two of these came in the last three games of the season. Indeed, the first eight away games were all lost, and the first away point didn't come until 21 November in a goal-less draw at Oxford. Even allowing for the fact that teams tended to be stronger at home then than they do nowadays (although there may be some statistics that disprove this claim, that is certainly the impression gleaned by a cursory look at League tables from this period), Swindon's away record was particularly poor. Why was this?

I don't know really why we were so poor away, although we hadn't been that good the previous season either. We should have done much better, because very often when a side is poor away from home the cause is a weak defence... but ours was excellent. Part of the problem was that we didn't bring any new players in, which was a mistake. I don't know who we would have changed, but you do need to bring in new players to keep things fresh and keep everyone on their toes. The other thing was that sides in the Second Division were getting used to us – often the second season is harder than the first, when you're an unknown quantity.

At home, the record was remarkably similar to the previous year. 1969/70 had seen them win thirteen, draw seven and lose only one game; 1970/71 would see one less win and one more defeat. Just three home defeats in two seasons. Indeed, if one includes 1968/69 and 1967/68, the team lost just six home League games in four years – a great achievement.

That was some record. You would always expect to lose two or three at home in any one season, just when you had an off day, so that is unbelievable really; no wonder we did so well. The crowd played a big part – they were so close to the pitch, especially before the new stand was built. I used to take the corners and I could sit on someone's lap to take them. I used to get lots of advice about what to do. Night games had a particularly great atmosphere – 20,000 packed in – I used to love that.

Don would finish top scorer again, with 16 League goals. Three times he scored twice in a match. It was a better return than the previous season, and, with his cup goals, he once again hit the magical 20 goals a season mark. What had changed?

> I don't know quite why the goals came back. Probably because we weren't playing as well, I had to take more responsibility for scoring, and tried to get inside the full-backs more, rather than always going outside the man.

Yet Swindon's season was ultimately a big disappointment after the successes of the previous year. The team that won at Wembley and had pushed so hard for promotion was beginning to break up. Neither John Smith or Roger Smart played in half of the League games and Don Heath had left. The team were overly reliant on the goals of Don, the ever-reliable Peter Noble, and Arthur Horsefield, who between them scored 42 of the team's 60 League goals.

> It was a difficult time; new players were coming in as some of the older players moved on, and without wishing to be unkind, they weren't as good as those they were replacing. We didn't have the money to go out and buy, so we had to rely on youngsters, who can take time to learn, and we weren't used to playing with them.

At his best, Don was still a match-winner, feared by his opponents and revered by his adoring home crowd, as this report makes clear.

Rogers Tips Scales
by Francis David

Swindon 3 Norwich 2

This enthralling battle in the sludge was won by the more elegantly imaginative side three minutes from time after Swindon had watched thunder-

struck while Norwich pulled back a two-goal deficit. Only the magic control of Don Rogers reminded them that this was a game they could win.

Few players in any league could have moved over the sodden turf with the speed of Rogers this rain-filled afternoon. Once he moved deep into the Norwich half with five defenders palpitating at his heels, and the rest of his team standing still in astonishment. Three of the pack were beaten with lazy abandon before his shot was scrambled away by goalkeeper Keelan.

Earlier, Rogers had scored an individual goal to put Swindon two up, and his generalship was the plus-factor which finally took Swindon further up Division Two after nine games without defeat.

The only black mark to both teams on this difficult pitch went to Norwich 'keeper Keelan. Porter's inswinging corner was his, unchallenged by the near post, but he dropped the ball and Gough, Swindon's clever inside forward, returned a desperate clearance for Burrows to give Swindon the lead with a massive drive just under the bar.

Foggo ghosted free several times on the right, but the Norwich front-runners, Paddon and Howard, couldn't win the ball in the air. Seconds before half-time came a hint of a Norwich revival: Paddon's corner was headed by Silvester towards the far corner of the net and only a brilliant saving header by Thomas prevented a goal.

When Rogers dribbled around Keelan to make it 2-0 in the 48th minute, Swindon seemed to have avoided any further embarrassment.

Yet in the 66th minute, Paddon's free kick on the left was pushed back by Foggo and Anderson tapped it over the muddy line with Swindon's defence marooned. Eight minutes later, Livermore picked up Silvester's cross to score what looked like another simple goal.

The 15,000 crowd roared for Rogers to redress the balance and he obliged. Loitering in a space, he dribbled Swindon back on to the offensive and set up the winning goal. It came clinically enough from a set-piece corner: Porter crossed and Noble out-jumped everybody to head inside the far post.

Norwich's tiny forwards deserved a point for ceaseless endeavour and without Rogers might have taken two.

Swindon: Downsborough; Thomas, Trollope, Butler, Burrows, Harland, Porter, Gough, Horsefield, Noble, Rogers. Sub: Smith

Norwich: Keelan; Payne, Black, Stringer, Govier, Anderson, Livermore, Silvester, Howard, Paddon, Foggo. Sub: Briggs

The highlight of the season yet again came in the cup. The FA Cup, after a victory at Queens Park Rangers in the third round took them to a tie at Elland Road, Leeds. The Yorkshire side had been too strong the previous season when playing away; at home it was very one-sided as the Town slumped to a 4-0 defeat as Don recalls:

> We never had a chance. It was hard enough playing them the previously season, when we were going well; but to play them away when we couldn't win an away game – not a hope! I never got anything against Leeds in my career. They were my bogey side, I think you can say!

The best night of the season came in the League Cup. On 6 October, Bill Shankly's Liverpool came to the County Ground. They left having been beaten by 2-0, Don scoring both of the goals:

> I scored two decent goals that night. The first was a one-on-one with the 'keeper where I knocked it round him and put it in, and then the second was a side-footed volley from a cross by John Trollope – for some reason I was on the right when he crossed from the left. Bill Shankly said afterwards we were lucky to win! That result just showed that we could still win the big games, but we probably needed a full team to do it.

His left-sided colleague remembers the game for a slightly different reason: 'I crossed the ball for Don's second goal, and as I did so my hamstring went! Don ran them ragged though, and, although they weren't quite the side they were in the later part of the '70s, they were still a very good side.'

The papers were clear about the matchwinner. Headlines such as 'Hero Rogers mobbed as Liverpool crash', 'Salute Giant-Killer Rogers', 'It's King Rogers', 'It's Don Destroyer' and 'Rogers is Swindon knock-out' adorned the following morning papers, along with this report from Norman Fox in *The Times*.

ROGERS SWEEPS LIVERPOOL TO DEFEAT
by Norman Fox
(The Times)

Swindon Town 2 Liverpool 0

Liverpool, never at their best against smaller clubs, and Swindon Town, never better than when pitted against big clubs, were both as good as their reputations last night when Don Rogers swept Liverpool out of the Football League Cup at the third-round stage.

Rogers finished Liverpool with that spark of brilliance that has burned so brightly for Swindon in so many memorable cup occasions. After a quiet first half he suddenly came alive with two magnificent goals in two minutes.

Swindon people had feared that their side's prolonged inability to finish well-constructed moves would jeopardise their chances. Certainly the tendency to make Rogers the commander overall, even when he was in no position to use his skills, almost seemed to hinder their promise until he found his true speed and confidence in the second half.

Lloyd, the immensely strong and reliable new pinnacle in the Liverpool defence, and the steely Smith found Rogers' early work no more than an irritation. Yet in spite of Heighway's ceaseless trying and the fiery tenacity of Evans, the Liverpool attack clearly missed the speed of Graham. Only twice in the whole of the first half did Heighway and Evans make the Swindon defence creak and strain, and on both occasions, around the thirtieth minute, their shots hurtled narrowly past.

The game drifted into mellowed expectancy – a finely balanced stalemate that the young men of Liverpool accepted with obvious reluctance and increasing concern. Even the more match-hardened Hughes fell short of his own standards with a complacent pass that was intercepted by Rogers, who pummelled a shot straight into Clemence. Whether it was remorse or annoyance that revived Rogers makes no difference; he was suddenly inspired to score twice, in the 65th and 67th minutes.

Noble's precise clearance sent Trollope on a thirty-yard sprint down the wing and his cross pass dropped at the feet of Rogers. Moving across the goal, he took Clemence with him until the gap widened at the far post and then he struck. Meanwhile, Trollope lay injured after his exertions and that superb pass which made the goal was his last of the game.

Dangerfield substituted, and it was his pass out of defence which sent Rogers on his race for the second goal. Again, he moved across the face of the goal, seemed to have played into the goalkeeper's hands by narrowing the angle, and then screwed the ball back into the net.

That finished Liverpool. But Dangerfield was still not convinced. He crashed a shot against the crossbar to send the First Division victims back to Anfield with no doubts why Swindon are an extraordinary cup side.

Swindon Town: R. Jones; R. Thomas, N. Trollope (sub: D. Dangerfield), J. Butler, F. Burrows, S. Harland, J. Smith, A. Gough, A. Horsefield, P. Noble, D. Rogers.

Liverpool: R. Clemence; C. Lawler, A. Lindsay, T. Smith, L. Lloyd, E. Hughes, B. Hall, A. Evans, S. Heighway, D. Livermore, J. Whitham.

In the context of the season though, any away draw was likely to be a problem, and a trip to Second Division Fulham in the third round proved to be the team's undoing as the hosts won 1-0. It summed up the season: great at home, awful away.

Not even the 'glamour' of the Anglo-Italian Cup could save the campaign. The side narrowly failed to reach the final again, finishing second among the English teams, but fewer than 10,000 saw the two home games at the end of May – a draw with Bologna and a comfortable home win over Sampdoria. The end of May was usually a time when most footballers are thinking of their summer holidays. Did Don and his colleagues think the tournament was a waste of time?

> Not really, because it was enjoyable to play against different teams and on different grounds. We played at some great places in Italy over the two seasons we competed. The weather was good, and the trips to Italy were good fun, regardless of the football, so we didn't mind still playing in May.

The big news of the season came in April. On 8 April, the board decided to sign Dave Mackay, the former Scottish international, from Derby County for £20,000. Note that the board decided, not the manager. There was a very good reason for this. The board had decided that Mackay, to quote Mattick, 'should be responsible for the training and the selection of the first team, with a view to his becoming team manager in the 1972/73 season.' Fred Ford, the existing manager, was to be offered the post of chief scout. The board further decided that 'The team should be strengthened but the wage bill reduced'. Brilliant.

Now it should be clear to anyone who has read thus far that this is not a book that seeks to 'dish the dirt' on all and sundry. Don is simply not like that; he is a genuine man who looks for positives in others, not negatives. However, it would be fair to say that of all the people I spoke to Don about, Dave Mackay was the person about whom Don was the least warm, and a little guarded in what he said: 'At the time we thought it was a good move – a very good player coming into the club. He would be a good asset to us. We did wonder where Stan Harland was going to play though..'

In the event, Mackay declined to act as manager until the 1972/73 season, so Ford remained in charge. It must have been an odd time at the club:

Fred wasn't very happy about it at all; particularly when Dave Mackay brought in Des Anderson as his own right-hand man. I think it was all wrong looking back on it, but at the time, as a player, you don't think about it. Your job is to play, and you get on with it. It wasn't a happy time at the club. ·

All this was in the future when Don was the subject of a major profile in Marshall Cavendish's *Book of Football* in the summer of 1971. The profile, which contrasted him with former Swindon winger Mike Summerbee, now a major star at Manchester City, was entitled 'Swindon's home and away winners'. In the article, Bert Head was quoted as describing Don as 'introspective' and gave his view as to why the winger was still at Swindon: 'You have to know his parents for one thing. His mother was a really lively woman. His father was quiet and reserved, and Don took after him.'

Joe Mercer, who tried to sign Don for Manchester City, gave his view:

I don't know Rogers too well, but from what I have seen on him on the field, he is more like a Bobby Charlton. Even if the stand is threatening to collapse, he just goes on playing football in his own sweet way as if nothing else were happening around him. He certainly is a talented player, most skilful, and able to take defenders on and go round them and score goals.

Former manager Danny Williams was quoted as saying: 'You have to push him hard in training to get the best from him on Saturday. I used to give him stamina training. He didn't like it but he was a better player for it. Although he has been capped at under-23 level, he's good enough to walk into the full England team.'

The profile goes on to say:

Arsenal are said to be one of several clubs who would speed westwards if ever Swindon finally decided to sell their star player, and one of his famous extra-time goals is still discussed at Highbury.

His physical contribution to a game and his work-rate are rationed because, as an artist, he believes only in the virtues of skilful attack and, as the local hero, can afford to leave the chasing to others.

His stay at the club has obviously been influenced by other factors: his genuine attachment to the town of Swindon, his interest in his sports shop where he spends nearly all his free time, his marriage to a Swindon-loving girl and his gratitude to a club that has given him, if not lasting wealth, then security beyond concern.

The article ends with an unerring prediction of the future 'Rogers, an early developer, may be a late mover, like Ivor Allchurch, who did not leave unfashionable Swansea Town for Newcastle United until he was in his late twenties. He was not too late to leave his imprint at much higher levels. Perhaps this will be Rogers' future too.

Rogers may want to remain a one-club man. But if he were to leave to spend his final seasons in one of soccer's Meccas, it would be safe to bet that one day he will return to re-settle in the Swindon of which he is so much a part.'

Many would agree with that assessment – Rod Thomas for example, who left Swindon a year after Don, would say that Don got 'too comfortable at Swindon'. Other teammates would echo that view. All say that he was to leave Swindon too late on his career, although they recognise that this was not entirely down to him.

Given the state of the club, season 1971/72 started with probably less optimism than any other for many years, as Don is honest enough to admit:

It was a very difficult time at the club. Players were starting to move on, and the calibre of players coming in weren't as good as those leaving. I think at the start of the season we knew we weren't going to be challenging for promotion, which was the first time for many seasons that we had thought that.

A 4-1 defeat at Blackpool, newly relegated from the First Division (with Don scoring the Swindon goal), seemed to point to a hard season ahead, but then the team went on a run of just one defeat in the next seven. That statement is a 'glass half-full' one, as in fact only two of the seven were won, but the side looked remarkably solid – just two goals were conceded in those seven games. This was no doubt influenced by the presence of Dave Mackay, who lined up at the back alongside Frank Burrows, with Stan Harland moving into midfield.

> I'm not surprised we didn't concede many goals. Stan in midfield would have been more defensively minded and that would have helped, even though he was out of position. Putting Stan in midfield didn't help Dave Mackay with the players though, because Stan was our captain, and had played brilliantly at the back for many years, and then he lost his place. Stan wasn't happy about it, and he soon left to join Birmingham.

It was another false dawn. The next ten games saw just one win, and more worryingly only four goals (and one of those was an own goal!). Towards the end of this run, there was the inevitable management change. After a 1-0 home defeat by Middlesbrough on 30 October, the board decided to dispense with the services of Fred Ford. Mackay was now given free reign, as the Club's official manager. History records very few successful outcomes, in any field of life, where there is more than one leader, and so it proved here. It clearly was no shock to the players, as Don explains:

> It wasn't a surprise and I think Fred was so fed up with what was happening that he was happy to go. I think he was treated very badly by the club, but at least he was so well liked in the game we knew he'd get another job.

1 *Above:* A young Don studies a Dudley Moore record with great interest. (Don Rogers)

2 *Below:* Don warms up in front of the old Shrivenham Road stand. (EMPICS)

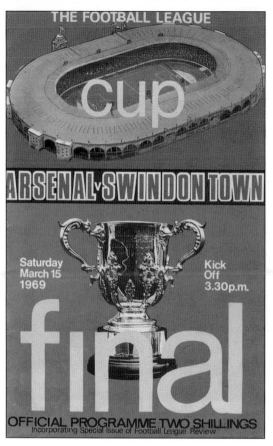

THE FOOTBALL LEAGUE

cup

ARSENAL·SWINDON TOWN

Saturday
March 15
1969

Kick
Off
3.30p.m.

final

OFFICIAL PROGRAMME TWO SHILLINGS
Incorporating Special Issue of Football League Review

3 *Left:* The programme from Don's greatest day in football – Swindon *v.* Arsenal, 15 March 1969.

4 *Below:* The full staff of Swindon Town Football Club, both playing and non-playing, line up before the big day at Wembley. (EMPICS)

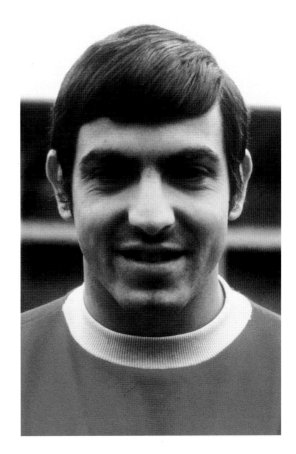

5   *Right:* Don in 1969, in a press shot taken for the final. (EMPICS)

6   *Below:* After the game; Don holds the cup while reliving the game. (EMPICS)

7   *Opposite:* Don Rogers, 1970. (Don Rogers)

8   *Above:* Don with club captain Stan Harland. By now the trademark moustache is present! (Don Rogers)

9   *Right:* Experienced pro; Don towards the end of his first spell at Swindon. (EMPICS)

10   *Above:* Don in action on his Palace debut against Everton. (EMPICS)

11   *Below:* Don scores the debut goal that made him an immediate crowd favourite – Palace *v.* Everton 1972. (EMPICS)

12   *Above:* ... and with goalkeeper David Lawson sitting disconsolately on the ground, celebrates his goal. (EMPICS)

13   *Below:* More celebrations for the new boy. (EMPICS)

14 *Above:* Don in action during the famous '5-0' game between Palace and Manchester United. (EMPICS)

15 *Below:* Don scores one of his two goals in that Manchester United game. (EMPICS)

16   *Above:* Don scores for Palace against Southampton. (EMPICS)

17   *Below:* Deadly from a yard. Don practices with his great friend Alan Whittle, 1973. (EMPICS)

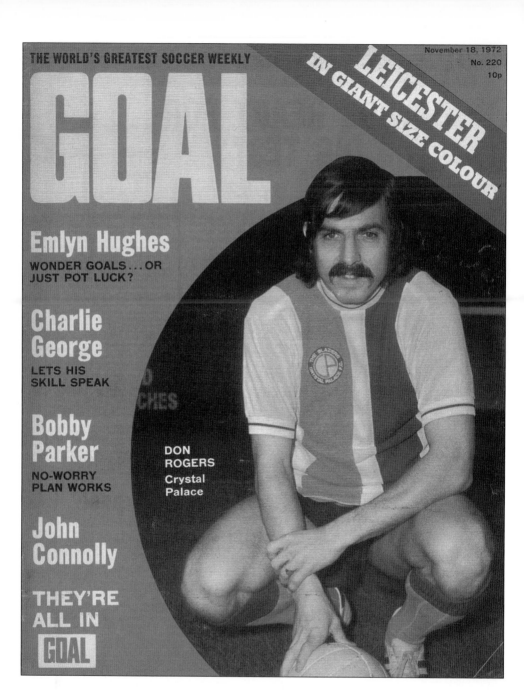

THE WORLD'S GREATEST SOCCER WEEKLY

GOAL

November 18, 1972
No. 220
10p

LEICESTER IN GIANT SIZE COLOUR

Emlyn Hughes
WONDER GOALS... OR
JUST POT LUCK?

Charlie George
LETS HIS
SKILL SPEAK

Bobby Parker
NO-WORRY
PLAN WORKS

DON
ROGERS
Crystal
Palace

John Connolly

THEY'RE
ALL IN
GOAL

18 *Above:* Cover man. Don on the front cover of *Goal* magazine 1972. (EMPICS)

19 *Opposite:* Family man; Don with wife Jane and daughters Emma and Lucy. (Don Rogers)

20   Proof that even thirty years ago, footballers could be persuaded to pose for pictures in ways they might later regret! Here Don is pictured during the heady first season with Palace. (Don Rogers)

21   ... and appears here to be cooking a football. (Don Rogers)

Don Rogers a MUST for a full cap

LAST OCTOBER Palace manager Bert Head made the best buy of 1972. He stole silently away to

ROGERS—YOU'RE MAN FOR ENGLAND

All yours, Rogers

'HE'S A MUST FOR ENGLAND'

Rogers must be capped

22 *Above:* A selection of headlines as the papers try to get Don into the England side during his first season with Palace.

23 *Right:* Don prepares for his second season with Palace, 1973. (EMPICS)

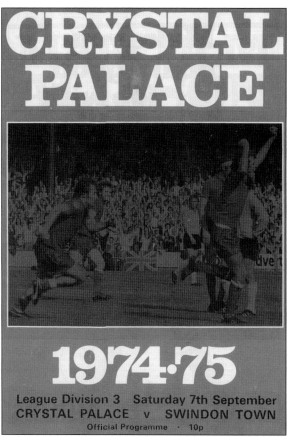

CRYSTAL PALACE

1974·75

League Division 3   Saturday 7th September
CRYSTAL PALACE   v   SWINDON TOWN
Official Programme   ·   10p

24   *Above:* Don trains with Malcolm Allison, the manager for much of his time at Palace. (EMPICS)

25   *Left:* End of an era. The programme cover for Don's last game for Palace, ironically against his first club, 1974.

26 *Above:* A rare shot of Don as a QPR player, 1975. (EMPICS)

27 *Right:* Don has always been a great ambassador for football within the Swindon area. Here he presents a trophy to a young player, shortly after his retirement from football, 1977. (Don Rogers)

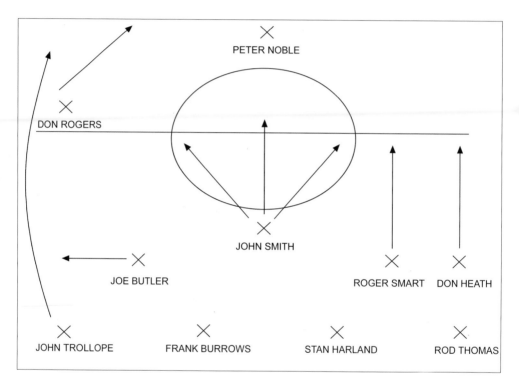

28 How Swindon's tactics worked, 1969. Don plays as the second striker, and stays on the wing, cutting infield when gaps appear. John Trollope joins him on the left wing as an overlapping full-back, and Joe Butler covers for him. As a result of this formation and the work rate of the midfield players, Don is given space to cause havoc! (From a diagram drawn by Frank Burrows)

So what was life like under Mackay? Don's pause speaks volumes:

> He didn't say much to me to be honest. He rarely spoke to me. I
> just don't think he came over well to the players, although it's a
> long time ago now. The players didn't gel with him like they'd
> done with Danny or Fred. To be fair to him though, he was player-
> manager, which was a tough job, and the team was doing badly, so
> it wasn't a good time.

Although it was a difficult time, Rod Thomas, later to play under
Mackay again at Derby County, and to win a League
Championship medal there, was keen to point out that both
Mackay, and his assistant Des Anderson, were big fans of Don: 'Dave
Mackay was a great admirer of Don. I think he recognised the skill
and talent and decided to let Don get on with it. Des Anderson was
the same, and was an excellent judge of Don. I remember a game at
Fulham when Don got the ball in space on the halfway line, and
Des said "He'll score here", which is exactly what happened.'

When Ford left, Swindon were in fifteenth position, but they
recovered to finish eleventh. The away record was better, with five
wins, but conversely there were five home defeats – the most
since the relegation season of 1964/65. On their day, the team
were still capable of turning on the style. For example, over the
Christmas and New Year period they scored seven goals in two
games against Portsmouth and Fulham, Don contributing four
of them, but overall it was a season that confirmed Swindon as
now no more than just a mid-table Second Division side. The
club that Don had joined in the early 1960s would have been
delighted with this, but not the one that had aspirations of First
Division football.

> It was a mediocre season, and the problem was that we simply
> didn't have any money to bring in good quality new players – it
> was all going on the stand. Of course now, we'd say it was one of

the best things the club ever did when you look at all the corporate facilities there, but at the time it was a real millstone – it crippled the club. Everything can go downhill in football very quickly: no money for players, poor performances on the pitch, lower crowds, less money – it's a tough business.

For Don personally this was not a great season. Despite those four goals in two games, he only scored three others all season. His tally of 7 League goals was his lowest since his first full season, 1963/64.

I think a lot of it was down to the fact that I didn't enjoy the season at all. It was my unhappiest time in all my years at Swindon. If you're not enjoying your football, at any level, you're not going to play so well. It was a bad time for the club – not really anybody's fault, but it was no fun.

The biggest match of the season took place in the FA Cup, where the third-round draws gave Swindon a home tie with Arsenal. Inevitably, the media made much of the rematch of 1969 and all the attention focused on Don. It was welcome respite from a difficult season, and reminded the wider football public that Don was still alive and well. Bob Wilson, previewing the match for *Goal* noted that 'Don has this unique ability to pop up as a match-winner', while Don himself was quoted as saying: 'The League Cup final was the biggest moment of my career. Unfortunately this season the goals have been eluding me. The chances have been there but I haven't taken them. It would be nice to start off again when we face Arsenal.'

The game itself, watched by Swindon's record attendance of 32,000, was a disappointment. There was no rerun of 1969 as the visitors won comfortably enough by 2-0. 'I don't remember that – can you believe it? Probably because we lost, but I cannot recall anything about the game – 32,000 in the ground, the place must have been buzzing!'

Don was now about to start his eleventh season at Swindon. No longer were his club going to be challenging for promotion to the top flight; if Don was to play in the First Division it would have to be via a transfer: 'That summer I can remember being really worried about what sort of season we were going to have. I knew we weren't good enough, and couldn't see how we could change things without money, which of course we didn't have.'

It was a sticky start and only two of the first twelve games were won. The side was in major transitional period: Peter Downsborough, Rod Thomas, John Trollope, Joe Butler, Frank Burrows, Roger Smart and Don himself from the class of '69 remained, but for Downsborough and Smart this was to be their final season at the club. The same was true for Don.

> It was very sad to see a once great side struggling. We were a shadow of our former selves, and it was very difficult to take. You look back and think 'if only', and in this case it was all about not bringing in enough new players to get things going again and prevent staleness. If we had done this a couple of years earlier, I don't think we would have been in that position, because the team would have been better, the gates would have been higher, and the financial position might have not been so grim.

Not only were matters on the pitch causing concern, off the pitch there were major problems. The problem was the new North Stand, or to be more precise the repayments on what was supposed to have been a development that would signify how serious Swindon as a club were to progress still further. With Mattick recording the club as losing £1,500 a week, the entire playing staff was put up for sale in October. How aware were the players of the financial situation?

> We knew the club was losing money. They'd built a new stand and couldn't afford to pay for it, so something had to change. Even now, because Dave Mackay has a bad reputation at Swindon,

people come up to me and say 'That Mackay, what was he doing selling you?' and I have to tell them that it was nothing to do with him – it was down to the board, not the manager.

With all due respect to the other players, Swindon's two most marketable assets were Rod Thomas and Don Rogers. Understandably the board were keener to sell Thomas: while the Welsh international full-back was undoubtedly a quality player, he lacked the idol status that Don enjoyed, within the club, with the support, and in the town itself. It wasn't to be, however, although Thomas would be sold a year later to Derby County, where he would go on to win a League Championship medal (ironically under the management of Dave Mackay). This time the only offer was for Don.

'Bert Head came round and saw me. I think the board set him up, because he made no effort to hide it. He came and parked his car outside my house. That was when I realised that I might leave – until then I assumed that they wouldn't let me go. I think that it was only because I was the only one who anybody offered decent money for that they sold me.'

John Trollope recalls: 'It was a time of real unrest for everybody at the club, and I think there was an inevitability that someone would have to go, and Donald was the main player so it was always likely that he would be the one.'

Don played his 400th League game for the club in the 2-2 draw at home to Brighton on 28 October 1972. Later that evening he was transferred to Crystal Palace for a fee of around £150,000 (£150,000 is the fee generally quoted, although Mattick gives the figure as £147,000). To put the fee into perspective, the British transfer record at that stage was £225,000. It was a lot of money for a Second Division player, but it shows how valuable Don was seen to be.

Don says it all happened so quickly:

I had seen Bert, so I knew he was interested, but didn't know what was happening – you didn't get told much in those days. Anyway, I was in the bath after the Brighton game and someone came down and said 'You're wanted upstairs'. So I went up to where the board were meeting, and discovered they'd had an emergency meeting at which they had agreed to accept an offer from Palace, and they wanted to know whether I was happy to go. So I said to them 'I need to think about this', and they sent me away to think about it into a small room opposite where they were meeting, and said they needed a decision that night. So I went into this room, all by myself; everyone else had gone home, and had to make a decision. Luckily Jane and I had discussed what we might do if Bert's interest came to anything, so I was able to say that yes, I would go.

At Palace, he would be reunited with the man who had given him his League debut, Bert Head. 'In the end, I suppose it was quite an easy decision to go. I wasn't really enjoying my football and it was a chance to work with Bert again, who of course was a known quantity to me. I must admit I didn't know where Palace were in the table though – I can assure you that's true – although had I known that they were bottom, it wouldn't have changed my decision. I felt that if Swindon wanted to sell me, and that someone wanted to buy me, then I might as well go.'

Both John Trollope and Frank Burrows were surprised that there wasn't more interest. Here are John Trollope's thoughts:

> I thought that once people knew he was available there would be a bit of a rush, but I'm not sure there was as much interest as I expected. Maybe with us as a team not playing so well it worked against him. Although Palace were a good club, they weren't one of the very best. I think though that if you look at football a lot of players go to where a previous manager is, and I am sure Don felt happy that he would know Bert Head at Palace, so that may have influenced things.

Frank Burrows comments are similar: 'I did expect more interest. I think people looked at his age – twenty-seven or so – and thought it was too much of a gamble to spend £150,000, which was a lot of money back then. I guess Bert was prepared to buy him, because he knew what to expect.'

So, Don's time at Swindon was over, temporarily as it turned out. For ten years he had been the star of the show, and had been the player with whom football fans would associate the name 'Swindon Town'. He had seen the side secure success that it could only have dreamed of when he first joined the club in the early 1960s, and he had played a huge part.

For John Trollope, it was a sad day: 'It was the end of an era really. I'd played behind him for ten years, and knew him really well. He was my roommate when we went away, and we used to go out together with our wives. I think I knew it would happen one day, but it was still a sad day.'

Don's own views echo this sentiment:

It was in many ways a very sad day, because I'd been there for so long, and it was my club – the only place I'd ever played. I knew everyone, and until the last year or so, I'd had a great time. I must admit I had mixed emotions when I finally signed – excited about the First Division of course, but certainly a sense of loss about what I was leaving.

The Best Player
in the Country

Don left one struggling side for another. Crystal Palace were bottom of the First Division. Struggling was something the London club were used to; they had found the going tough in the top flight of English football since their promotion in 1969.

This was Palace's first ever spell in the First Division, and although we may now think of them as a 'yo-yo' club, alternating between the new Championship (although called Division One when they last graced it) and the Premiership, in fact their history until the 1970s was very similar to Swindon's. Apart from a brief spell in the 1920s, they spent much of their time in the old Third Division (South). Indeed, just over fifteen years before Don joined them, they finished one place off the bottom of that league (Swindon finished bottom), and when the regionalised Third Divisions came together to form the new Third and Fourth Divisions in 1958, Palace were in the Fourth Division.

Promotion to the Third soon followed, however, and there was a further promotion two years later (the year after Swindon had been promoted to the Second Division). Although they were not in relegation trouble over the next four seasons, they were never closer to the top than seventh (in the days when there were only two sides promoted and no play-offs), and it was a major achievement when promotion was achieved to the First Division in 1969, the same year as Swindon moved back up to the Second.

Since promotion, Palace had finished twentieth, eighteenth and twentieth, narrowly surviving relegation on each occasion. Now, as Don joined them, fifteen games into the new season, they were bottom, and had only taken one point from their previous eight games. Bert Head had already been active in the transfer market: within the space of four days in September he had signed Scottish defender Iain Phillip from Dundee for £105,000, Irish full-back Paddy Mulligan from Chelsea for £75,000, and another winger, the mercurial Charlie Cooke, also from Chelsea for £85,000. Back then, £265,000 was a lot of money! In fact it could have been more, because in the middle of his spending spree, Head had also put in a bid, reported to be £100,000 and two players, for another top talent in the lower leagues, the Bournemouth centre forward Ted MacDougall. The bid was rejected and the next day MacDougall joined Manchester United for £200,000.

The Palace club historian is the Reverend Nigel Sands, and he put this time in Palace's history into context: 'Palace were really struggling. It had been a dreadful start. They badly needed a goalscorer to keep them afloat. Bert Head, at that time, was spending money to try and patch things up, but he still, until Don was signed, was looking for a goalscorer.'

Don immediately noticed the differences between his old club and his new club:

> The first thing that struck me was the size of the players' car park – it was so much bigger than at Swindon – there was space for sixty or seventy cars. It was a Monday when I arrived, which meant that, with Bert Head as manager, it would be a practice match, because Bert always used to like doing that on a Monday, particularly if you'd lost on the Saturday. However, there were so many players at Palace that there were two full-scale practice matches. Imagine that,

forty-four players at least on the club's books, and I think they were all professionals! Off the pitch things were different as well – one of the best bits was being able to just leave your training kit on the floor: at Swindon we had to take it home and wash it ourselves.

There seemed to be immediate pressure on Don to perform. Not only was he Palace's record signing, and expected to make a difference to their League form, but he was signed as an entertainer – somebody who could lift both the crowd and his own team. Don though, is dismissive of any such suggestion:

> I can honestly say that I didn't feel under pressure, and I didn't worry about the size of the fee – that wasn't down to me, and all I could do was to perform on the pitch as best I could. The pressure was more off the pitch, because early on we were still living in Swindon, so I was driving there and back each day to training – two hours each way – that was hard.

Nigel Sands says Palace's expectations of Don were very clear: 'Don was signed to score goals. He had an excellent record at Swindon in that respect, and had become known, not just as a winger, but as someone who scored.' Don's new (or perhaps to be more precise, old) manager, Bert Head, was clear that he had made a great signing, being quoted in *Goal* as saying:

> I'm absolutely delighted. I brought him to Swindon as a fifteen-year-old, and I am confident he can play a big part in our future. We never really thought he would become available, but when we heard he was, we moved in straight away. Don is a top-class player, and I am sure that he will do even better in the First Division than he has in the Second.

Don, for his part was no less delighted about the prospect of his First Division debut, being quoted in the same magazine as saying: 'I have spent the past ten years hoping I would play in the First

Division. I have always wanted to play there, but quite honestly I had almost given up hope.'

In *The Daily Mail* he wrote:

When a club has already spent a lot of money and is at the bottom, paying a six-figure fee for somebody else is obviously a gamble. But in a way joining Palace is a gamble for me. For ten years I've been dying to get into the First Division and I'm sick of all the rubbish about me not really being ambitious enough to want to play in the big league.

Don's debut for his new club was on 4 November 1972, at home to Everton. It was a game that was to make him an instant hero to Palace fans, as he scored the only goal (and how) in a 1-0 win. However, the impact of that goal, cutting in from the wing to score, was far greater than just in London, SE25. The game was televised by BBC's *Match of the Day* and Don's goal was therefore transmitted across the UK (I can still remember the thrill of seeing 'our Don' on national television), and a star was born.

I was very lucky to score a good goal in that first game, because that got me in with the crowd, the press, and the players – and we won as well, which always helps. From my point of view, it was the type of goal I had been scoring regularly, but the Palace fans said they'd never seen a goal like it. My big memory, though, is after the game – we had arranged to go to The Bell at Ramsbury for a meal in the evening, and the people that ran the place let us go upstairs to their own lounge and watch the game on the television in the evening – they served us coffee upstairs while we were watching! The other thing I remember about the game was that Alan Whittle was playing for Everton, and he and our centre half, Mel Blyth, had a right set-to on the pitch… and then he came and joined us later that season.

ROGERS REPAYS TRADER HEAD

by Brian Glanville
(The Sunday Times)

Crystal Palace 1 Everton 0

Crystal Palace, those wheelers and dealers of the bleak South Eastern world, may at times look more like second-hand car dealers than a football club, but it is still too early to dismiss them. Yesterday, beating an Everton side which should have made a meal of them, it was quite clear that they have bought some gifted players with all that money. Trader Head, as one might call him, is at least and at last gambling on skill and quality, in the shape of Rogers and Cooke.

Cooke, as we know is one of the most mesmerising enigmas, Rogers one of the great lost talents of their era. The goal with which Rogers, who has wilfully been hiding his light under a bushel at Swindon, won the game, showed him at his powerful, fluent, best. Like Cooke, that beguiling strategist and ball player, he is a footballer of glorious natural gifts who has threatened too often to deceive.

Rogers, who seemed determined to see out his career at Swindon, cost £150,000, Cooke £80,000, Phillip, who looked only a moderate midfield player, £110,000, Mulligan, who had a mercurial game, £70,000.

But however well the money proves to have been spent, there are still weaknesses in the team, in midfield, in the back four. Besides, in spite of the spirit evident yesterday, both method and motivation remain in doubt. Nor can the team afford the sort of idiotically gratuitous foul which got Blyth sent off 14 minutes from time, after flooring Whittle when the ball was out of play.

Since we're discussing money, it is also pertinent to ask how well Everton have invested in Belfitt, so weak yesterday in the air, and in Bernard. For £140,000 one is entitled to expect more than a brisk opening 20 minutes.

Palace's beginning was shaky; slow recovery and poor positional play got them into all kinds of trouble. Scarcely had Hurst's casual back-pass brought Lawson rushing from his goal than the excellent Jackson, at the other end, had a still closer call. Bernard won the ball at a throw in, in his own half, and clouted it perfectly for Belfitt to chase. With Bell ponderously heavy on the turn, the centre forward had a clear run on goal, but out of his area came Jackson to beat him with a fine tackle.

At another throw, Taylor's slack positioning let in Whittle on the right. His cross was struck twice by Belfitt, first against Bell, then at Jackson.

We had 22 minutes of this type of thing and were beginning to feel embarrassed by and for Palace, when what should they do but break away for a delightful goal. Craven, receiving the ball in midfield, turned on it and stroked in cleverly into the path of Rogers. The expensive new winger, who had only just forsaken his beloved left touchline for the right, ran on, calm and irresistible, to thump the ball past Lawson.

Belfitt should have equalised only two minutes later, were it not for monumental carelessness. Mulligan's own fallibility had let in Connolly on the left when there seemed to be no danger. Connolly crossed over Jackson's head, the goal lay open, but Belfitt contrived to head across and past it. How very badly Everton miss Royle.

With Kenyon long off the field with a cut eye, and the Everton defence relying too much on off-side tactics, Palace were well into the game. A splendidly lobbed pass by Cooke to the massive Hughes threatened a second goal, but Kendall got in his saving tackle. When Kenyon returned, it was immediately after a long shot by Payne had sailed over Lawson and bounced of the top of the bar.

Everton's response was a shot on the turn by Connolly, which Jackson got a desperate hand to at the near-post to concede a corner, a feat he repeated when Connolly later shot again from still nearer range.

Soon after half-time, Jackson was diving again, this time to a shot by the irrepressible blond, Whittle, whose speed, sharpness and courage make him such a dreadful thorn in the side of any defence. But it remained a game of strange mistakes, and just as Mulligan had let in Connolly, so Connolly now let in Mulligan, whose shot was headed out of the goal-mouth by Hurst with Lawson stranded.

Then, with Blyth very properly off the field – and most inappropriately applauded by the crowd as he went – Everton hadn't the bite or wit to *retrieve the game. Indeed, they might have lost another goal when Craven's shirt was pulled in the box, just as Mr Burtenshaw tactfully blew the final whistle.*

Crystal Palace: Jackson, Mulligan, Taylor, Phillip, Bell, Blyth, Hughes, Payne, Craven, Cooke, Rogers.

Everton: Lawson, Scott, Newton, Kendall, Kenyon, Hurst, Whittle, Bernard, Belfitt, Harvey, Connolly.

Palace fan Peter Gee, writing in the fans' history of Crystal Palace *We all follow the Palace*, recalls the Don Rogers signing and impact:

> At last here was a player with the potential to excite the fans. We were not to be disappointed. The big clubs had shied away from him, perhaps unsure whether he could step up to the grade. We'd seen him on television on a number of occasions and he looked the business, and we all remembered him racing across the mud scoring Swindon's third goal in the 1969 League Cup final against Arsenal. Rogers had seemed comfortable at Swindon and to step up at twenty-eight [although in fact he was only twenty-seven] appeared to be a couple of years too late. On the evidence of the first twenty minutes of his Palace debut against Everton it appeared our money had been misplaced. My dad was already moaning when it happened. Put away by John Craven, Rogers outpaced the Everton defence and, one-on-one against 'keeper David Lawson, calmly chipped home.

Inevitably it was all smiles after the match. Bert Head said: 'He had a dream debut and scored a smashing goal. But this is what we've paid money for. I'm sure Don will score a lot more goals for us. We have bought a jewel. Don Rogers can be poetry in motion. Give him the ball and he will change a game for you. We want to let Don get on with it. He has already shown that he has the skill to turn a game. We want him to function as a natural winger, to use his natural initiative and talent. You can't restrict a Don Rogers, you must let him play. Give him the ball and let him take it from there.'

Don was equally pleased:

> That goal did me the world of good. As soon as I received the ball from John Craven, I made my mind up to head straight for the goal. But at the end of the game I felt dead beat. The pace of the game was easily two yards faster than what I've been used to with Swindon in the Second Division. I feel as if I could do with a week's rest.

Alan Whittle, soon to be Don's teammate, was on the opposing side that day: 'I'm sure Don would admit that we dominated the game and should have won! The problem was that we couldn't score, and of course, Don could. It was an excellent goal, and typical of the man – he was so good one-on-one – and the goal, running through the middle, was what I guess you'd call his "trademark". Don was so strong and quick – he really could cover the ground, and once he was away, nobody was going to stop him.'

Don remembers the week after the game, as the press (in much the same way as they do today), decided that a new star had been born:

> The week after the Everton game was crazy. All the papers wanted to talk to me – and of course it was all on a different scale than I had been used to, because there were so many of them. Some of the stuff they wrote was ridiculous really – Palace find a new hero and all that kind of stuff – and I'd only played one game! In the end I joined the press myself – I used to write a regular column for the local Croydon paper.

The next game was away at Derby, the team who were the reigning League Champions. The Rogers bandwagon gathered momentum as he scored again in a 2-2 draw.

It was another goal that was a bit like my 'trademark' goal really – a ball through the centre and I ran on to it, and rounded the 'keeper. That was a good result for us up there because Derby were a very good side and would have expected to have beaten us.

At the time, Don was quoted as saying 'I thought I would be doing well to score two goals by Christmas, so it's nice to get two goals in my first two games'. The national papers were in their element. Headlines such as 'New boy Rogers stuns Derby' and 'Rogers does it again' were the inevitable result of Don's goal. 'What a goal for "King" Don' wrote Arthur Hopkins in *The Sunday Mirror*.

Don had now been at Palace for two games. He was, however, already a national star. The front cover of *Goal* for 18 November 1972 carried a colour picture of Don. Thirty years on I show it to him again, and it brings a smile and the comment that 'I've signed more of that front cover than anything else. I must have signed hundreds of them!' Ken Jones, one of the foremost football writers of the day, used his column in the same magazine to extol Don's virtues: 'Crystal Palace could not have ordered a better start from their new winger Don Rogers than a match-winning goal and sustained proof of the man's stirring individuality. It happened exactly how Palace must have hoped it would. A sudden break. Murderous acceleration. Admirable calm under pressure. Faultless finishing. The stuff which £150,000 attackers should be made of.

He is trying his luck in the First Division, when there is suddenly more scope for players who have the talent to turn a defence out of traditional situations. Rogers looks eager to take defenders on, looking to bypass them with his pace and effective control. Like others of his kind he should be encouraged.

Don Rogers may have left it too late for personal glory. But the football he is playing suggests that he is not entirely defaulting as an international prospect. If he can keep it up. If he can prove that industry is part of his make up, we could yet see him in an England jersey!'

The next match was at home to Don Revie's Leeds United, then the foremost side in the country, although perhaps just starting to show signs of decline. Don had played them before, of course, in successive seasons in the FA Cup while at Swindon, but never in a First Division fixture. Palace should have won. They led 2-0 at the interval, both goals from John Craven – 'inspired' according to one report by Don – but were pegged back to 2-2, with Mick Jones and Johnny Giles scoring for the visitors.

I enjoyed that one, although we should have won, having been 2-0 up. I think part of it was down to belief. I'm not sure we could believe we were ahead at half-time, and in the second half they played very, very well, and deserved a draw. It was tough though. I know things went incredibly well for me, but I did find it harder, mainly because all the players were so much quicker than at the level I had been used to playing, so the game itself was much faster. Having said that, the thing that helped me was that they gave you more room – they think they can play, so they focus on that, and if you can play you've got a chance because there's more space.

Everyone wanted a piece of Don. Dick Mattick kindly lent me a book of cuttings taken from newspaper articles to supplement my own magazine articles. The book shows that Don was being inter-viewed all the time. In one article he admitted: 'I wish I was surer of myself. Sometimes, when I go out there, I feel that no matter how hard I try, things won't work out. It comes to me quickly once I am out on the pitch. It's not something that happens to me frequently and I don't worry about it, simply because there is nothing I can do. Maybe one game out of six or seven this mood comes over me. Football is a game of confidence. One day you believe you can run through a team, the next you are struggling to beat one man.'

The next two Palace fixtures produced only one point – a draw at Chelsea was followed by a narrow defeat at Ipswich, Don's first in a Palace jersey, but then came the match that to Palace fans is still one of the most famous in their entire history: the game against Manchester United at Selhurst Park on 16 December 1972.

United were not a great side at that stage in their history, and arrived at Selhurst Park in some disarray. Palace may have returned to the bottom of the table after the defeat at Ipswich, but United were only just above them in twentieth position. The great European Cup-winning team of 1968 was being broken up, and that era's most famous stars – Denis Law, Bobby Charlton and George Best – were all coming to the end of their United careers. Law and Charlton were fading as age caught up with them (Charlton would retire at the end of the season, and Law would also leave United at the end of the season for one last year at Manchester City) and George Best, because… well no-one quite knew at the time. What was fact was that Best had been dropped by Frank O'Farrell the United manager for missing training, and would not feature at Selhurst Park (in fact he would not play again that season, and would only play a further dozen games for United). So this was a side in transition, but no one quite expected what followed.

United were thrashed 5-0, as Palace, and Don in particular, ran amok. Don scored two, and was instrumental in everything his side did, as they tore their opponents apart. As with the Everton game, this one was on nationwide TV – and it had a huge impact in making Don a star.

ROGERS SHATTERS A SAD UNITED
by Brian Glanville
(The Sunday Times)

Crystal Palace 5 Manchester United 0

On the basis of this dreadful performance, one can only say that Manchester United's bizarre decision to give George Best yet another chance, looks the fruit of utter desperation. Nothing in their past, simplistic treatment of the problem suggests that they are any closer to a solution, while the effect on morale, especially, if they have gone over their manager's head may be imagined. Yesterday it appeared low enough already.

Best's case, which surely now verges on the clinical, has been ludicrously misunderstood at both ends of the spectrum. On the one hand there are what one might call the floggers and hangers, who believe that if he only got his hair cut and went to bed at 9.00 p.m. like Stanley Matthews, all would be well. On the other hand are the bleeding hearts who feel that to such genius, every possible indulgence must be shown.

Crystal Palace, who have bought with such shrewdness, and yesterday added the electric Whittle to their already coruscating ranks, were largely allowed to frolic as they pleased. United's odd choice not to substitute the injured Dunne for so long after the first goal helped to precipitate the rot. Palace, in that spell, might have scored two or three others. United's weakness may be gauged by the fact that though the home team squandered chance after chance, they were still able, in due time, to pick up four other goals.

Though they played so elegantly and well, there was an unreality about the occasion which must inhibit judgement on Palace. Not often will Cooke have so much room and time to exhibit his outstanding repertoire. Not every week will there be a defence so pitifully easy to split, so abjectly vulnerable to the searing bursts of Rogers, the muscular excursions of Hughes. Rogers played ducks and drakes with United, using his pace, his power, his often exceptional eye for an opening. Payne and Phillip also did their share of probing, while Whittle, as the game wore on, became increasingly a menace.

In United's tattered ranks, Moore ran occasionally with force and courage, Law had a header or two, Stepney kept the score down, Morgan persevered but — even allowing for Charlton's absence — there is no pattern or balance to the side. Kidd, playing deeper than usual, Davies and MacDougall are three strikers in search of an orchestrator.

After Stepney had saved easily from Hughes, and Moore had struck Jackson's legs after Dunne's lob disconcerted Palace, the home team scored in ten minutes. Rogers' glorious pass inside the back sent Mulligan racing in at a sharp angle on the right, to beat Stepney with his low drive.

Dunne now hobbled off the field, and United tottered. Rogers shot just wide of a post, Payne cleverly put Whittle through for a shot, which Stepney bravely turned over; Blyth, moving on to Cooke's delicate return, wastefully shot too high. United were in such a state of bemusement that you wondered why it was so long before Law at last appeared, dancing impatiently on the line, to watch as Hughes went round two men, and Stepney grabbed Whittle's point-blank shot in mid-air. Law, once on, played in midfield, Young at left-back.

MacDougall sharply heading in a rebound, to be given offside, reminded Palace that to waste chances is to tempt disaster. Three minutes from half-time, they roused themselves to score again; and again, it was Mulligan. Rogers was the true architect, superb acceleration winning him the ball on the right, after he'd given the defence several yards. When the ball came back to him, he laid it cunningly to Mulligan, who again shot hard and true.

Immediately after half-time, Whittle put Rogers through, and the rest was formality.

There was a rare instant when United threatened a goal. Morgan glided round Payne on the left. Law, with a nostalgic unexpected header, putting it just over. Almost at once, however, United's sad defence opened again, Cooke sending Whittle through, Stepney saving once more.

With eight minutes left however, Whittle was off again. Hughes sturdily held his pass, returned it, and the blond little forward consummated his debut with a cross shot high into the right-hand corner. Five more minutes, a pass by Blyth, and again United's defence was as square as a brass band. Rogers, for the second time, did final execution.

I located a couple of other reports on the game. Sadly for our history of Don, while all play tribute to his performance – 'Rogers was tormentor in chief', 'Rogers outpaces United' – the reality is that for all the papers, just like *The Sunday Times*, the real story was as much United's demise as Palace's great win. However, that wasn't Don's concern:

It was a fantastic game, and it could have ended up with any score, because they had chances, but we missed some sitters too – Mel

Blyth missed one which was an open goal I remember. But it was what you want to see: lots of action in the box.

Personally, I think it was the best game of my career – I set up the first two goals for Paddy Mulligan, and then scored a couple myself. I could have had more as well – if you look at the video, I nearly scored in the first couple of minutes, then I curled one just over the bar when I probably should have scored. The two goals were very enjoyable: one I went round one side of the 'keeper, the other round the other side. The last goal was my favourite, because I took it so coolly, even though I say it myself. In fact when I look at it now I amaze myself. It is probably up there with one of the best goals I've ever scored, because I could have blasted it or lost my head, but I just side-footed it into the corner. Everyone liked the other goal, when I went round the 'keeper and put it in, but I preferred that one.

Again, I was lucky that the game was on the television. Somebody said to me the other day that whenever I did anything really good it was always on the box – remember only a very few games were televised then. This one, the Everton game, the game against Stoke when I scored my best ever goal – the cameras were there for each one, which meant a lot more publicity. And from the Palace fans' point of view it was like they'd won the World Cup – beating Manchester United 5-0, it just didn't happen.

Every Palace fan of a certain age will remember this game, which Nigel Sands describes as 'one of the best results in the club's history'. Sands recalls:

Don was brilliant that day. He didn't just score two goals, both of which were great individual goals, but he set the others up. I think that was the day when he became a Palace hero – although United weren't a great side, it was still incredible for a team like Palace to beat them 5-0!

Peter Gee recalls that game: 'Rogers simply ran riot against poor United, laying on two first half goals for Paddy Mulligan before scoring two individual goals of the highest class, with an Alan Whittle goal in between.'

As the match report explains, this was Alan Whittle's debut for Palace. The blond striker had been signed from Everton, and he and Don soon became firm friends:

Don and I were staying at the Norfolk Court Hotel, and the manager there was a guy called Charles Taylor, who owned a gleaming Rolls-Royce. Anyway, I decided it would be great to turn up for my debut in it, so I asked him if I could borrow it. When he said yes, I roped in Don and we went up to Selhurst Park for the United game in it together. It was like we were movie stars – the fans couldn't believe it, and you could see them just staring at us. Some of them asked us whose car it was, and I told them it was Don's – his present for signing on!

The game was incredible, absolutely astonishing. I know United weren't very good, but we took them apart, and Don was at the heart of everything, because he wasn't just a great goalscorer, he was a supremely talented all-round footballer.

The immediate aftermath was significant for United. Frank O' Farrell was sacked three days later; on the same day, George Best announced his retirement from football. As one moustachioed winger faded from the scene, another, it seemed, was taking his place as one of the most exciting talents in the country.

Meanwhile, the Don Rogers bandwagon moved on to a fixture at Leicester where Palace, despite Don's goal, lost 2-1. Three days later on Boxing Day, Palace beat Southampton 3-0 at Selhurst Park. Don scored twice more, which meant he had now scored five times in his last three games, and seven times in his first eight games for the club. Talk about an instant impact…

Things just seemed to go well from the start, and I couldn't have asked for any more – everything was as you would have wanted it to happen. I don't know whether it was because people weren't used to wingers running through the centre – if you look at the two Manchester United goals, for example, I've not run outside the defenders, I've run inside them, and shot from in front of the middle of the goal.

By now the papers were clear. Don Rogers should be playing for England. After the Southampton victory, one headline read 'King Don for England'; another said 'Don Rogers ranks as the most exciting individualist in the Football League'. By the end of the year, with the papers previewing Palace's game at Anfield, the bandwagon hadn't just started, it was out of control. 'Rogers waits for Sir Alf' said the *Daily Express*, quoting Don as saying 'it would be tremendous even to be in the position where Sir Alf might have to take notice'. 'Rogers: the man who has put the sparkle back into soccer' said the *Daily Mail*. Even the more sober Brian Glanville, writing in the *Sunday Times* wondered whether Don was 'what our international team needed', even if amusingly he quotes Don's teammate Paddy Mulligan as saying that 'Don's the type of player you need to keep talking to; if you neglect him for ten or fifteen minutes he can relapse into Disneyland.'

After that purple patch, Palace went three League games without a goal, although Don did score in another win over Southampton during that period, as the South Coast side lost again at Selhurst Park – this time 2-0 in the FA Cup. After the game, the visiting manager, Ted Bates, was fulsome in his praise of Don, as was the former Charlton goalkeeper Sam Bartram, now writing for the *News of the World*: 'Don Rogers for England? Yes, it should happen! On this display nobody at present in the England side can match him as a potential match winner.'

Ted Bates, the Southampton manager told the assembled press: 'He must be the best player in the country. I rate him as the finest forward in the country today. I also believe he should be playing for England.'

Don's own manager was equally forthright: 'How can you leave a player like Don out of the England side? He's fantastic.'

With hindsight, this game marked the absolute highpoint of Don's Palace career. By now the papers had completely gone overboard – it is no exaggeration when you read the press after this game to talk of 'Rogersmania' and to compare the press with that given to Wayne Rooney in the summer of 2004. Headlines after the Southampton cup-tie included 'Super Don', 'Rogers must be capped', 'All yours, Don' and 'Rogers – you're man for England'.

Below is the type of article that was appearing at this time.

ALAN HOBY'S COLUMN
Don Rogers a MUST for a full cap

Last October, Palace manager Bert Head made the best buy of 1972. He stole silently away to Wiltshire and paid £155,000 for a shy, spry, wing genius called Don Rogers.

At the time, many scoffed. After ten years of Second and Third Division football with Swindon, Rogers' move – they felt – had come too late.

At twenty-seven, he had become too complacent, too comfortable in his footballing ways. With his West Country burr and easy-going approach, he lacked ambition, drive. Owner of two sports shops and a building business, he had settled for second-best, for security, for being king of the local goldfish bowl...

But how wrong the cynics were!

You cannot kill talent. You cannot destroy technique. You cannot suppress style, class, ball-playing magic.

Head, another West Countryman knew this. He knew because, as Swindon's manager more than a decade ago, he signed Rogers as an apprentice. Don, from the Somerset hamlet of Farrington Gurney (pop. 646) was just fifteen.

But, from that point onwards, it was clear to all who saw him that here was a young footballer of rare grace and skill. Amid the stern prose of so much League soccer, he brought a touch of poetry.

As he matured and the years peeled off, he won two England under-23 caps. And when in 1969 little Swindon beat Arsenal 3-1 in the League Cup final at Wembley, Rogers, the two-goal star, took to the big occasion like a duck to water.

All this Head remembered when, just over two months ago, he went back to the County Ground: and Swindon, who needed the cash, at last consented to sell.

Since then Don Rogers has routed his critics by scoring eight goals in ten games. Whether he was running inside to the long diagonal pass, or whether it was the effortless control he showed when the ball was laid off to his feet, he proved he was a thoroughbred.

He ran straight at rattled opponents. He outpaced defenders. He startled goalkeepers by feinting one way before slotting home on the other side. He brought a new glamour and excitement, not only to Palace, but wherever he went. He was the game's new hero. As Head said 'I never doubted for a moment his ability to make the transition to the First Division. He is such a cool customer when he gets in front of goal. Nothing flusters him.'

The Rogers qualities – artistry, thrilling acceleration, change of pace, and deadly finishing – are of course, precisely the qualities that Sir Alf Ramsey's stereotyped, wing-less England need so badly.

With his long hair, sideburns, and Mexican bandit moustache, the Palace striker is an individualist who can yet play within the framework of the team. He is a prime example of how individual skill can beat the system and the robots.

'After being at Swindon' he says, 'playing at Palace before a 30,000 crowd is like playing in the Cup Final at Wembley in every match. The atmosphere lifts you.'

What then would the England atmosphere do for him? Dave Mackay, Swindon's former chief, who sold Rogers to Palace, has no doubts. Mackay, now manager of Forest told me: 'He is a tremendous player. The only thing you have to remember is that he is a very quiet, modest lad. He would never go about shooting his mouth off if he was not picked by Ramsey. But he has the skill, and is certainly good enough to play for England.'

Will Alf Ramsey take the hint on Tuesday when he announces his squad for England's return World Cup clash against Wales at Wembley on Wednesday week?

He should. He most emphatically should, if, in the long run, we are to have any chance at all of winning the World Cup next year in Munich (that is if we qualify!).

For too long England teams have bored us with their drab defensive efficiency, their brawny strength, their plodding predictability. It is time we stopped living in our own little world of self-delusion. We have enough hard, honest labourers in English football to fill a factory.

What we need, what in particular, England needs, are more players with the skill and subtlety of Gunther Netzer, the shooting power of Gerd Müller – or as near as we can get to them.

Don Rogers, I am convinced, comes into this special category. What the England team needs are GOALS and Rogers would bring an element of much-needed surprise to the attack. All he requires – like most artists – is encouragement.

So what's about it Alf? What about playing the Palace ace against Wales? As Charlie Cooke says '*Don has brought a fresh eye to the game*'. And you never know, it might fill Wembley.

Don remembers the Southampton cup tie:

We played them twice in very quick succession and did well both times, as I recall. The goal I can really remember is one where I went round the goalkeeper, but he pushed me very wide and I had to try and knock it in from a very narrow angle – again that would be one of the best goals I've scored. I also remember scoring a header – I think it was in the cup-tie – John Craven headed it across goal, and I put it in.

Nigel Sands says it's hard to underestimate Don's impact: 'Don revitalised us in 1972/73 – not just because of his goals, but because of the way he played, particularly at Selhurst Park. He made an incredible impact straightaway and lifted the whole club; putting both the team and himself firmly in the limelight.'

By now *Jimmy Hill's Football Weekly* had ceased publication, but Jimmy Hill himself was now writing a regular column for *Goal*. In the 20 January edition he wrote in praise of the man who was most definitely the player of the moment: 'Such is the power of Rogers that he appears to accelerate past people even when he is slowing down. I can't remember a player who, when clean through with the ball at his feet, has Rogers' ability to pull away from chasing defenders, even the quick ones. Bert Head tells me that he has never really seen Don sprint full out in training; he never needs to because he is always well ahead of the other players in second gear.'

Back to the England situation. Despite all the press coverage and the lobbying on his behalf, Sir Alf would not be moved, as Jeff Powell had predicted in an article written on the day of the squad announcement for the World Cup qualifying tie with Wales at Wembley under the headline 'Rogers is no cert with Alf'. Powell wrote that 'Sir Alf Ramsey takes a chance with all the ready enthusiasm of a Presbyterian minister who has wandered, absent-mindedly into a Las Vegas gambling palace'. Don was not chosen. His best chance had gone, as he now accepts: 'The real chance I had was for that Welsh match. I was playing well and I had all the press on my side – some of things they wrote were incredible really. That was the moment for Sir Alf to take a chance on me, but he stayed loyal to his existing team.'

Don scored again in the FA Cup fourth round, but in vain, as Sheffield Wednesday produced a major shock by knocking Palace out after two draws by virtue of a 3-2 second replay win (in the days when those games happened) at Villa Park, scene of another second-replay disappointment for Don six years earlier. The focus though was on First Division survival, and when two successive games were won in February, away at West Bromwich Albion, and at home to Stoke (another goal for Don), Palace were up to seventeenth, and in the days of only two clubs going down, starting to pull away from the dreaded drop zone.

Let's go back to the Stoke game. The words 'another goal for Don' do not really do justice to what happened...

> The first thing about the goal was that I won the ball from a Stoke defender. I know that sounds very hard to believe, but it is on the video! I've come back about twenty yards from our goal and played it to Alan Whittle, and then run out to the left wing to get the ball back, and then just run past players before I put it in. It was voted ITV's Goal of the Season, although one bloke on the panel, a football journalist called Bernard Joy, said I didn't mean to do it, which upset me! I was very proud to win that award because there were a lot of good goals scored in those days.

Alan Whittle was keen to pay tribute to the goal, but more specifically how Don played the game: 'I remember that goal well – it was Don at his very best, just running at people. They didn't know what to do. From my viewpoint, Don was great to play with, and we formed a good understanding. The ball used to be knocked up to me, and I knew that Don would never check his run – he'd just go, so if I could knock it in behind the defence he would be running on to it. Then one-on-one he was so good that you'd have a really good chance of a goal.'

Just before I started to write this book, I bid on a football memorabilia site for a video entitled *Vintage Crystal Palace: Six Classic Games from the Big Match*. Hopefully my wife will never read this, but I bid up to £15.00, only to be overbid by somebody who I hope was a Palace fan. Having now seen the video (Don lent me his copy), I wish I'd bid higher and won, for they show Don at his very best. He features in the first four games – Manchester United, Stoke and Chelsea from 1972/73, and Bristol City from 1973/74, all of which Palace won. In that video he scores a total of four goals, three of which are brilliant individual efforts, and makes most of the others. If anybody ever wants to see Don at his peak in the First Division, this is the video to watch.

The edition of *Goal* for the weekend of the Stoke match, Saturday 17 February 1973, carried a full-page feature on Don. It is a glowing profile; in retrospect this was the very height of Don's First Division days, and possibly his whole career – Palace were improving and seemingly getting out of relegation trouble, and Don himself was at the forefront of everything good about their revival. It's worth quoting the article, written by Nick Harding, in full; this is the peak of Rogersmania.

ROGERS SPARKS TERROR FOR THE 'KEEPERS

There can have been few more terrifying sights for First Division goalkeepers this season than that of Don Rogers menacingly bearing down upon them. For there has been an almost uncanny certainty about the outcome every time the new idol of Crystal Palace fans has outstripped the last of the pursuing outfield defenders.

Seven times in Rogers' first ten games for his new club, he has coolly placed the ball beyond the advancing goalkeeper from such situations.

By doing that and heading another goal, only the third of his career, Rogers enhanced not only his own considerable reputation but also improved Palace's hopes of avoiding relegation. Yet how does he feel when placed in such a position of responsibility, the vital points so often depending on whether he can keep his head and deceive such goalkeepers as England internationals Peter Shilton and Alex Stepney.

'I make my mind up straight away' says Rogers. 'It's the first thing I think of – what I'm going to do when I get to the goalkeeper. Sometimes I decide to go round him, sometimes I push it past. Usually as soon as I get the ball I can tell if they're going to rush out or stay put. You have to decide as quick as you can. If you don't think what you're going to do, you can get in a hell of a tangle. When I was younger I remember a couple of times when I didn't make up my mind, and as a result didn't score. I suppose you learn from experience.'

Those who can still recall Rogers' two great goals, which helped Swindon destroy Arsenal during the extra-time period of the 1969 Football League Cup final, will certainly testify to that. It was goals like that which made Rogers such a favourite with the West Country club. Two coachloads of supporters still continue to see him in action, travelling to every Palace home game.

And now at last it's not just before his team's home crowd that Rogers impresses. He can turn it on in away games as well, which didn't happen so often while he was playing in the Second Division. He was sometimes criticised for that and says: 'Maybe it was true. I was disinterested without realising it. But now I enjoy playing away. We have to raise our game every week as every game is a big one'.

He is also eager to put right those rumours that have suggested he was content to play out the rest of his career at the County Ground: 'I asked for a move three times and each time they said "no" and I couldn't do a thing about it. I didn't even get to hear if other clubs were making bids for me, but I did want to get away' Rogers stresses.

He finally did get away when, with their gates falling drastically, Swindon decided they would recoup by selling either Rogers or Welsh full-back Rod Thomas. When Palace manager Bert Head and then chairman Arthur Wait made an immediate move, it was thought that their target was Thomas, but they disproved that theory by paying £150,000 for Rogers who had previously been under Head at Swindon.

Says Rogers: 'I didn't give it a thought that Palace were at the bottom of the First Division at the time, neither do I give a thought now to the possibility of the club going down. We won't do that. No, what decided me was the way the manager was talking. He said he was going to spend a lot more money on players and he's been doing that.'

Head certainly kept his promise in that direction. For £90,000 Alan Whittle and £115,000 Derek Posse followed close on the heels of Rogers, who had also been preceded at Selhurst Park by other big-money signings in Charlie Cooke, Paddy Mulligan and Iain Phillip.

But Rogers is keen to emphasise that no one player, not even himself, should take too much credit for his goals and Palace's revival. 'I think most of them have put passes through to me that have led to goals. Charlie's put me through, Iain did, so did John Craven and Alan Whittle' he says, going through almost half of the Palace team.

Not surprisingly, Head himself has been overwhelmed by the success of Rogers, who at long last has given goal-starved Palace fans something to cheer in recent weeks.

'Of course we were delighted that Don got off to such a good start' enthused the Palace chief. 'He's a delightful boy, and both a manager's and a fan's ideal player. He's a thrilling player and worth a lot of money to watch when in full flight' Of Rogers' chances of being selected for England, Head comments: 'There is still a long way to go as I think Sir Alf Ramsey has kept faith with his established players. However, if Don continues like this, I am sure that Alf will consider him.'

Judging by the way the England attack struggled so woefully to beat down the reinforced Welsh rearguard in the recent Wembley shambles, it cannot be too long before Ramsey looks in Rogers' direction.

The England forward line is crying out for his kind of powerful, direct running which has had First Division goalkeepers – and defences – in a dither this season.

Clive Bettison at that stage was still playing for Lambourn Sports, but still made the effort to go and watch Don at Palace, mainly for night games. He remembers one incident which showed the impact Don was having:

> I went up to watch a night game at Selhurst Park, and on this occasion I drove. I wasn't sure of the best place to park, so I asked a Palace fan, who must have been in his early fifties. He came with us in the car to direct us, and when we got chatting I explained that I had come up from Swindon to watch Don. His reply was to say that 'I've been watching Palace for many years, but we've never had anyone like Don Rogers play for us before' – he was just in awe of the way Don had been playing.

Palace's improvement was to be a false dawn though. Just two points were taken from the next six games, four of which were at

Selhurst Park, to leave Palace back in trouble. More significant were matters off the pitch. On 20 March it was announced by chairman Ray Bloye that Bert Head would be promoted to general manager. Mr Bloye said 'Mr Head will be running the whole complex here. There has always been a gap between the board and the team manager, and this is a bid to fill it. Within the next few weeks, it is our intention to appoint a first-class team manager, who will set about planning for the 1973/74 season.'

In other words, Bert Head had been 'moved upstairs' as the football parlance goes. Effectively, he became one of the first ever people to hold what these days is referred to as the position of 'director of football'. Promotion... not likely! As he had been when Head left Swindon eight years earlier, Don was very surprised: 'We were all shocked by the decision, because although we'd had a bit of a slump, overall we were doing well, and playing some good stuff.'

The 'few weeks' referred to by Ray Bloye was in fact a week and a half. Ten days later, on 30 March 1973, Malcolm Allison was appointed as the new manager, on a salary reported to be £13,000 per annum plus bonuses (a big contract at a time when Don was earning £120 per week). Allison joined from Manchester City, where he had been hugely successful in partnership with Joe Mercer, bringing League, FA Cup, League Cup and European success to the Maine Road club. However, since the summer, when Allison had been in full control (as a result Mercer had moved to Coventry), things had not gone so well, as he made clear at his inaugural press conference: 'I am back home after spending eight years in the provinces. I had some happy times in Manchester, but recently my relationship with the players has soured – I couldn't motivate them. Palace is a club with vast potential and I am looking forward to the challenge.'

Don remembers the appointment well:

We were all sat in the dressing room, and were told 'your new manager will be here shortly'. None of us knew who it was going to be until Malcolm walked through the door. It was quite a surprise to us. We all knew of him of course, and he quickly put his ideas across. All he wanted to do was to play good football – pass and move. I think his downfall was that he changed the Palace team over too quickly, and we ended up with too many what I would call 'bread and butter' footballers. He was great company though, and I spent a lot of time with him.

Alan Whittle thinks that the management change cost Palace in the long run:

I was really surprised when they changed Bert Head during the season, because although we had lost a few games in the period after Christmas, I am sure it was going in the right direction. When Malcolm came in he changed things too quickly in my view, and as a result we suffered. Like Don, I still think we had the makings of a very good side indeed.

Allison's first match was Chelsea at home. Palace needed to win, and they duly did, with Iain Phillip and Jim Cannon scoring in front of nearly 40,000 at Selhurst Park. Don remembers taking the free-kick that led to Cannon's goal, and also the fact that Sir Alf Ramsay was in the stands watching – who knows who he was watching, but Don must have been one of the most likely ones. They remained twentieth, but with seven games to go, their fate was in their own hands.

It wasn't to be. Only one point was taken from the next five games, Don's penalty securing a 1-1 home draw with Ipswich on 14 April, after he had missed the previous game, a defeat by Manchester United at Old Trafford, because of the birth of his second daughter – although he was with the team he didn't play. Over the same period, Norwich City, in their first ever season in the First Division, and Palace's main rivals to avoid relegation, took five points. With two games to go, Norwich were two points ahead, but with a much inferior goal average (which was used rather than goal difference back then). The stage was set for both teams forty-first match of the season... Norwich against Crystal Palace at Carrow Road.

Back to the United game; Don may not have played, but he did help one of his teammates out, as Alan Whittle recalls:

After the game we went into Manchester and ended up at a night-club. Tommy Docherty was there, and as we had more to drink, he and I started to argue with each other over the game. I kept saying we were unlucky, and all he was saying was 'What was the score?' Anyway, in the end Don had to drag me away, because otherwise I would have got into a fight!

Don also helped me out at Norwich. We were mucking around in the hotel, and we let some of the fire extinguishers off, which set the alarm going, and all the fire doors started shutting. Everyone scarpered apart from me and I was left holding the extinguisher with foam everywhere. Don just appeared, grabbed me, and pulled me into his room to keep me out of trouble.

Back to the football at Norwich. It was a desperate night for Palace. Don scored from the penalty spot to give Palace the lead, but Norwich equalised before half-time. A 1-1 draw would have left Palace needing to win their last fixture and hope that Norwich lost theirs (which is in fact what happened), but in injury time David Stringer scored to give the home side a 2-1 win and send Palace down. It was one of the worst days of Don's career:

We shouldn't have lost. I remember that their equaliser should never have gone in – it was a header from a long way out, and we should have stopped it. I didn't feel under pressure for the penalty – I never minded taking them, and we should have built on that because we were the better side. It was the equaliser that knocked the stuffing out of us really.

It was an odd night, because after the game, as we were staying over, we went to a restaurant in Norwich, and Malcolm got them to put all the tables together in one long line, and we had effectively a 'relegation celebration' (according to his weekly column Don had whitebait and chicken breast stuffed with asparagus, if you're interested, which I suspect you might not be), which I know sounds strange, but Malcolm's attitude was that 'it's happened now, we can't change it, let's focus on next season.

The last game of the season took Allison back to his old club, and Palace signed off from the top flight with a 3-2 win over Manchester City. Don scored twice to finish the season with 13 League goals from 26 games – a tremendous record for a player in a relegated team, not to mention a winger playing for the first time in top-flight football. 'One goal every two games in a relegated side was a record I was very pleased with, and I was just so lucky to have such a good start, because everything seemed to take off from there. I really enjoyed it.'

Nigel Sands says that Palace were a little unlucky to go down, but knows the reason: 'The problem was that we didn't have anybody else other than Don who could score goals consistently. The next highest scorer behind Don, who of course only came in November, was John Craven with 7 goals. Teams knew that if they could stop Don from scoring then it was likely that Palace wouldn't score at all. If we had signed another goalscorer to play with Don, I am sure we would have stayed up.'

Martin Searle, also writing in the book *We all follow the Palace*, recalls Don's impact:

While Don was in the team we always felt that there was a chance of a goal as long as the ball reached the figure with the sideburns and the Mexican bandit moustache. He was capable of dribbling past whole defences on either wing or straight down the middle. Certainly every time he got the ball there was a palpable buzz around the ground.

Nigel Sands says that it was this half-season that has led to Don still, even to this day, being revered at Palace:

> Palace fans who saw him play that season, especially those who saw him every week at Selhurst Park, simply idolised him, and even now, they will still say that, just on the basis of those few months, he was one of the most exciting players to play for the club.

Further evidence of the high regard in which Don is still held at Palace came when I was writing this book. At one of our regular get-togethers, Don told me of an invitation that had come through for him and his wife to attend a testimonial match at Selhurst Park for a player 'he'd never played with and didn't really know'. It seemed simply that Palace wanted to keep in regular touch with one of their old heroes, who thirty years since he last kicked a ball for their club, was still in their minds.

After ten years of trying to get into the top flight of English football, Don's stay in the First Division had been short-lived, and he was back in the Second Division. There he would meet up again with his old team, Swindon, who, under new manager Les Allen, had flirted with relegation (they were as low as twenty-first after a home defeat by Oxford in February), but had survived for another season of Second Division football. It was a bitter blow for Don, having worked so hard to get into the top flight.

> It was a huge disappointment, because I'd waited so long to play in the First Division, and to then only have half a season was incredibly frustrating, particularly when I'd personally done well and enjoyed it. I still think we should have stayed up.

At the time there was some speculation that Don would leave, although in his weekly column he was quick to point out that he 'had no intention of rocking the Palace boat', despite the fact that he made no secret of his 'dislike of going back to the Second

Division and his hankering for life at the top.' At one stage it seemed that he might be encouraged to leave – one headline in a Sunday paper was 'Mal's axe may fall on Rogers' with the suggestion that Don only turned it on in home games; something he angrily denied at the time. Nevertheless, there does appear to be enough hard evidence, to quote Norman Giller in the summer of 1973, that 'Allison had mixed thoughts about Rogers the player at the end of last season.'

Looking back, Alan Whittle feels that Don should have left: 'I think there were a number of us, Don included, who should have moved on when we went down. We all wanted to play in the First Division, and in the end the only thing that kept us at Palace was the fact that Malcolm was so sure we would go straight back up, and we believed him. In fact, going down finished us as a side.'

In the close season Palace made history by becoming the first 'all-white team' to play an 'all-black team' in South Africa: 'Malcolm organised it all and it was a great trip. You did see some sights though because this was when apartheid was rife there. We went to one stadium where I swear there were only about sixty or so white faces and the rest were coloured.'

It was also important for Don on a professional level. He and Malcolm Allison got to know each other better, and Allison admitted that he 'had to reassess his view of Don as a player' saying that 'I did not realise he had such awareness – I dropped him back into midfield in South Africa and it really surprised me the way he was able to recognise situations quickly and turn them to the fullest advantage.' It was a theme Allison would return to before the end of the season, although he was also quoted as saying that Don would score 25 goals for Palace this season and be leading goalscorer in the Second Division, as well as 'guaranteeing' that he would win a place in the England squad!

Despite the relegation, there was a degree of optimism at Selhurst Park. True, this was in the pre-Premiership days, so there was no question of the 'parachute' TV payments that have helped so many clubs in recent years make an instant return to the top flight after relegation, but Palace, having spent so heavily in their bid to stay in the First Division, still had a very experienced squad for their new level of football. Confidence was high as they prepared to kick off their new season, and Don remembers feeling very upbeat: 'I was absolutely positive that we would be promoted straight back – I think we all were. We had some very good players, and we'd shown in the First Division that we were a match for anyone on our day.'

Alan Whittle agrees: 'It never occurred to us that we wouldn't get promoted. Everyone was very positive and we were sure we would only have one season out of the top flight.'
Palace's first game in the Second Division was at home to newly-promoted Notts County, when the Palace programme decided, on Malcolm Allison's instructions, to take the nicknames given to their South African opponents in the summer, and translate them into English. Don was 'The Troublemaker'. He duly gave his side the lead, but the visitors were equal by half-time, and then, sensationally, scored three goals without reply in the second half to give them a 4-1 win.

> It summed up the whole season that first half. We absolutely anni-hilated them – they didn't get a look in. We hit the bar or post four or five times, scored once and were all over them. Then we gave a stupid goal away – a goalkeeping clanger, when our 'keeper came out for a ball he should never have come for and it was 1-1 at half-time. I am sure, even now, that had we been leading 1-0 at half-time we would have won the game and the whole season would have been different.

It was a desperate start, and things were to get much, much worse. In their first fifteen League games, Palace failed to win, and gained just four points from four draws. The other eleven games were lost. It was, quite simply, an unbelievably poor beginning. To make matters worse, if things could be worse, Palace were also dumped out of the League Cup, losing 1-0 at Fourth Division Stockport,

who would finish bottom of the entire Football League at the end
of the season.

> Things went from bad to worse. We couldn't win a game, although
> we weren't that poor, which I know sounds stupid. We had no luck
> at all in some of the games, and we couldn't score at all.

In those first fifteen League games, Palace had scored just ten goals.
Don had scored six of them, including three in successive games in
mid-October. He was doing his bit, as Alan Whittle makes clear:
'Don was always a good goalscorer – it wasn't just his ability one-
on-one, but he had a very hard shot as well: his build meant there
was a lot of power there. He would always score goals,
regardless of where he was played, and I know Malcolm played him
in midfield for a while. The thing with Malcolm though was that
he kept changing his mind on what he wanted to do – at the start
of the season he decided that he'd make the pitch larger to help
Don, and then after we lost the first four games he made the pitch
smaller again!'

The first win finally came on 10 November when Alan Whittle's
goal gave Palace a 1-0 win at Bristol City, and this was followed by
two draws, including a 2-2 draw at Portsmouth where Don scored
twice, one from a penalty. That brought Don and his team to a
game that he had been looking forward to from the day the fixtures
were released – his first match against his old club, Swindon Town

'There was lots of publicity for that day, and it did feel a bit odd
playing against the team I'd played with for so long. Once the game
started though you want Palace to win, never mind Swindon, especially because of how our season was going.'

Swindon were in almost as bad a way as Palace. After a promising
start, where they won two and drew one of their opening three
games they had only won two games since, and were in twenty-
first place, with twelve points from their first eighteen games – four
points more that their hosts. By the end of the afternoon, that gap
was down to two, as Palace won 4-2. Inevitably, Don was heavily

involved in the entertainment, scoring Palace's first goal, which he describes as 'not much of a goal really.'

Any hopes that the win for Palace, their first home success of the season, and their fourth game without defeat, would spark a revival were short lived. Only two points, both from draws, and one goal in their next five matches meant that the Selhurst Park side entered the New Year still rock bottom. They were four points from safety – already, at this stage in the season, both they and Swindon seemed doomed, although Don says it didn't feel like that at the time: 'It was obvious we were in deep trouble, but you always think that you'll get out of it, particularly as we really didn't think we were that bad a side. You kept thinking that you'd get going and every-thing would be all right.'

Then, something changed. Don's goal gave them a 1-0 home win over West Bromwich Albion on New Year's Day, and this led to a run of eight wins, three draws and only two defeats in the first thirteen games of 1974 – promotion, not relegation, form. It was a remarkable turnaround and Don, with five goals in that spell, played a key role, as did experienced striker Derek Posse, with seven goals, and youngster Peter Taylor, a future England player and, briefly, England manager, with four goals.

> You see that was evidence that we weren't a bad side. It was a good run, and it was the type of run that we should have been able to go on with the talent in the side. I know I keep going on about it, but I am still amazed, even thirty years on, that we got relegated. It was stupid really.

Alan Whittle agrees: It was crazy really; the side, although Malcolm changed it too much to my mind, was way too good to go down. Some of the players were just too good for the division, and to get the best out of them they needed to be in the First Division.

After the 3-1 win at Fulham on Good Friday, 12 April 1974, Palace seemed to be pulling themselves clear of the relegation zone. They were now up to nineteenth, and although this was the first season of three up, three down (which meant that they were still only one place clear of the drop zone), they were the team in form, even if they were still only level on points with twentieth-placed Oxford United.

So Palace now had five games to play, two at home and three away. On paper they didn't look too daunting, with three fixtures against mid-table sides – Millwall, Fulham and Hull – followed by Don's first return to the County Ground against a doomed Swindon side, and then a final game of the season, a potentially decisive one, against relegation rivals Cardiff at Ninian Park.

The first three games were all lost. Critically, they included both home games, as both Fulham and Hull came to Selhurst Park and left with 2-0 wins. Palace were now back in the relegation zone.

'It was the same story as the previous season really – we seemed to have pulled ourselves clear, and whether we relaxed a bit I don't know, but we then lost silly games, against teams that we should have beaten, and suddenly we were back down in trouble.'

The stage was set for Don's return to Swindon. His previous club were already relegated, having won just seven games all season, and were at a very low ebb – just 4,655 had seen the previous home game against Blackpool. Yet, despite this, everybody wanted to see the Don's return:

> Everyone was very pleased to see me. I remember that, and I got a great ovation when I came out – because of course in those days the teams came out separately. It was good to go back, but as with the game against Swindon at Selhurst Park, once you are playing all you're focused on is winning for Crystal Palace.

In the event, the gate was nearly 12,000, Swindon's second highest gate of the season. They saw Palace win 1-0, Peter Taylor scoring the only goal, to apparently keep his side's hopes of avoiding relegation alive. However, once they got back to the dressing room those Palace hopes were rapidly dashed – points for their relegation rivals, Oxford, Cardiff and, most importantly, Sheffield Wednesday, meant that Palace were now staring relegation in the face.

Palace's last game of the season was at Cardiff. The vagaries of goal average meant that they needed to win by at least two clear goals to survive. They didn't threaten this and had to settle for a 1-1 draw. For the second successive season they were down. 'I don't remember much about the game at all. I think I must have blanked it out because it was such a bad memory. Two relegations in two years, and both of them should never have happened.'

Relegation from the First Division had not been entirely unexpected. Relegation to the Third Division was a huge shock.

> Nobody at the club could believe it – we did have good players, and those players don't become poor ones overnight, they really don't. Palace in the Third Division, when a year earlier we had been one of the most entertaining sides in the First Division.' I don't think it was just us who were surprised, I think most people in football were.

Nigel Sands says that, despite his goals, Don was less effective in the Second Division than he had been in the First: 'I seem to recall that Malcolm Allison withdrew him from being an out-and-out attacker and put him in midfield, where to my mind he was much less effective. Despite that he was still the leading goalscorer, which must say something!'

Nigel Sands does refer to an important point: Don played that season in a variety of positions for the club, no doubt partly due to the summer tour of South Africa.

> I played everywhere that season – that was down to Malcolm, who always wanted to experiment and try different things. He thought I was a good passer so he said that anyone who was a good passer could play in any position. His idea was to play me as a sort of deep-lying centre forward, with the wingers pushed up. I enjoyed it, although it took some getting used to.

Don nearly didn't see the season out with Palace:

> Dave Sexton tried to sign me for Chelsea in October. It was all agreed between the two clubs. The fee was going to be £200,000, and Sexton wanted me to play in midfield because of my range of passing – I think he'd seen me play there in a testimonial against Chelsea. Then on the Monday the deal was off: the Chelsea directors had had second thoughts about spending the money. I do wish I'd been able to have gone though. I would have missed Palace, but imagine playing at Chelsea every week with the team they had then. Still, who knows what would have happened given that Dave Sexton didn't last much longer as their manager.

The press at the time said that the deal fell through because Malcolm Allison got cold feet, saying that 'There will be no Rogers deal. I cannot afford to lose such a gifted player. It's true that I'm anxious to reshape the team... but the price of losing Rogers is too high.' Palace chairman Ray Bloye added 'If we sold Rogers to Chelsea, I would be lynched. He's one of our best blokes. We wouldn't swap him for two or three players (Palace were rumoured to be interested in Chelsea's Tommy Baldwin, Bill Garner and John Phillips). We would want the entire Chelsea team.'

Alan Whittle says it would have been a great move for Don: 'At that stage in his career, Don had to be playing in the First Division really. Chelsea would have suited him, although there were rumours that it was a bit of a closed shop there – cliques amongst the players, that sort of thing, so it might have been difficult for him to settle – who knows? Can you imagine it though, Don in the same side with people like Peter Osgood and Alan Hudson. It would have been great to have watched them.'

This was also the season that Don's hip problems, which would ultimately cause him to retire from the game, started:

> I got clobbered in one game, and it took a while to heal, so I went and saw the physio for an X-ray, because they couldn't work out

what was happening. When he saw me with the results, he told me to sit down, and said I had a major problem with my hip, and would need a hip replacement quite soon. He told me I should stop playing there and then, although he said that he knew that I wouldn't. He was right about the hip replacement though – the first one was done in 1979 – and he was right about the injury: I started to notice that it was slowing me down.

The club was in turmoil as it prepared for its first season in the Third Division since 1964. For Don, it was a disaster. He was now, at the age of twenty-eight, back in the division where he had started his career.

> It took a long time to sink in. Palace were such a big club that there was no way that they should have been playing in Third Division. All the players thought they were good enough to play at a higher level, and although we believed we would go back up, we'd thought that the previous season. For me personally it was very disappointing; although I loved Palace as a club, I really didn't want to play in at that level given the stage of my career that I was at.

Although Malcolm Allison was still the Palace manager, this was a very different Palace side from the one that Don had joined less than two years earlier. Gone were two of the big-money signings who had joined around the same time as Don – Iain Phillip and Charlie Cooke – and some evidence of the degree of transition was that Palace would use twenty-eight players in that season, a huge number in the days of only one substitute, and no squad rotation.

Don started the opening game of the season – a 1-0 defeat at Brighton on 17 August 1974 – and also began the home win against Tranmere a week later. He was substituted before the end though, and missed the 3-1 defeat at Halifax a week later.

The following Saturday he was on the bench for what proved to be his final game for Palace. Perhaps fittingly, it was against Swindon at Selhurst Park. Swindon, like Palace, newly relegated, were under new management, or perhaps we should say old management – Danny Williams had returned for a second spell at the club.

The match was very one-sided. Palace were 5-0 up at half-time and eventually ran out 6-2 winners. Don came on as a substitute for Ron Barry, although the game was long since won:

> Swindon were terrible in the first half, although I do seem to recall we played well. At that stage you would have thought that we would have finished way ahead of them in the table, but in fact if you look at the final positions, I think Swindon were the higher-placed team.

A week later, on 14 September 1974, Don left for Queens Park Rangers with Terry Venables and Ian Evans going in the other direction. After 69 full appearances in the League, and 28 League goals, Don's spell at Palace was over.

> I knew it was coming. There had been quite a bit of talk about me leaving, and I knew Palace wanted to do a deal to try and get Terry Venables in. I do remember the conversations with our physio before I went – he basically said that I was going because my hip was worse than Terry Venables' ankle and Ian Evans' knee!
>
> At the time I thought it was a great move. We didn't have to move house, and QPR had a reputation as being a very good foot-balling side, with some excellent players. I was back in the First Division, which I was delighted with, and I remember being very excited about making a new start.

Nigel Sands says, that, from a Palace point of view, Don's departure was greeted with an air of resignation, along with the expected sadness: 'Of course we were sorry to see Don go, but the truth was that it was inevitable given the relegation to the Third. I think there was also a sense that we might have seen the best of him as well – although we didn't know the fact that he was struggling with injury then, it seemed like the days of him flying down the wing were coming to an end, and of course Malcolm Allison had been playing him in midfield anyway.'

Don left Palace as a hero. Even now Palace fans of the 1970s still talk of him as an all-time hero, who illuminated what were two awful seasons for their club. As for Don, how would he sum up his at two years at Selhurst?

> My time at Palace was superb really, particularly considering that I played in two relegation teams. I got on very well with the crowd, which really helped, and I think I was lucky that they hadn't seen the type of wing play that I was able to give them, especially in that first season. I loved playing in front of the Selhurst Park crowd, and I think they knew it. Despite the fact that the team didn't do so well, from a personal point of view, it was a great time for me. I still wish we had stayed in the First Division that first season though, because I am convinced that we would have kicked on from there.

One final reflection on the 'Palace Era' – something that Don also mentioned in our discussions. There has been a recent trend for supporters to buy 'retro' replica kits: a reminder of bygone eras. The leading supplier of these types of jerseys is TOFFS (The Old Fashioned Football Shirts Company, in case you are interested). Their current catalogue has a plethora of shirts, including English and foreign club sides as well as international sides. For the English team selection there are over 150 shirts to chose from; all apart from one are denoted by the name of the club who once wore the shirt, and the season(s) they wore it. The exception is Crystal Palace 1972. Under this shirt is the name 'Don Rogers' (readers who want to see evidence of this go to www.toffs.com). To have a shirt named after you, perhaps that is the ultimate accolade; it is at the very least further proof of the impact Don had. Craig, in the business development team at Toffs, says the shirt has always been a good seller.

So Don was back in the First Division, Queens Park Rangers got a proven First Division goalscorer and goal creator, and Palace got a hugely experienced midfield general and a very promising defender in exchange to help them rebuild. It seemed like a good deal for everybody. For Palace it was to be an excellent trade – Venables would indeed play a key role for the club, although ultimately more as a successful manager, whereas Evans would play well over 100 games. For Don and QPR, however, the deal would be less of a success.

Don Rogers –
The England Story

Some sporting phrases seem designed to irritate. They are meant as a compliment to their recipient, but in fact merely damn with faint praise. 'Best player never to win a major' is one from the world of golf, the football equivalent is 'Best player never to play for his country'. Somehow the effect of this statement is to draw attention not to the 'best player' part of the sentence, but more the 'never played for his country' part. Great player, but…

So let's not use a phrase like this about Don. True, he never did play for the full England side, but he did play for them at other levels: youth and (as it was then) Under-23 level. A remarkable achievement for someone who spent virtually all his career playing outside the top flight of English football.

The first opportunity young players get to play for their country is by representing England schoolboys. This, surprisingly, is not a great indicator of whether a player is going to have a long and distinguished career – many players play for their country at this level and then fade away out of the game; conversely, many famous players never played international football at this age. Don fell into the latter category: 'I played for Somerset schoolboys, but I never got close to the England side. I was invited down to a big trial, but I didn't get any further than that.'

From there, the next step up was the Under-18s – the England youth side. Arguably this was the level at which Don had the greatest impact for his national side. He remembers his selection well:

> What used to happen in those days was that we were nominated by our clubs. I was put forward, and went to a trial, and then was selected after that. I was already in the first team, and I'm sure that made a difference – most of that England youth team were already in their respective first teams. We used to play at Roehampton, and report to the FA at Lancaster Gate.

The coach in those days was Wilf McGuinness, the former Manchester United player, whose career had been cruelly cut short by serious injury. He would later manage the Old Trafford club, albeit briefly, and Don was grateful for some good advice early on.

> Wilf was great. He used to mix really well, and I learnt a lot from him. We had lots of get-togethers that year, so I spent quite a bit of time with him. I remember one game at San Sebastian where I'd been clean through three times in the first half with the 'keeper to beat, and put the ball wide each time. At half-time Wilf came over, and said to me, 'When you look up and see the 'keeper coming out towards you, if you actually aim at the goalkeeper, then he won't be there by the time the ball gets there'. He's absolutely right – if you look at the television in a game, nine times out of ten, the goalkeeper has moved. I thought that was really clever, and if you look at my goals, you'll see I've often put the ball where the 'keeper was.

The whole of the England youth season was geared to one thing, the international tournament in Holland at the end of the season. The squad went away regularly. Spain was the first trip – to Murcia – and Don recalls that he 'travelled across Spain on the train overnight and didn't get any sleep – absolutely horrible!'

As well as playing internationally, the side also played against Manchester United's youth team at Old Trafford, where Don was to reappear, as we have seen, with his club youth side later that season. Don's first appearance at Old Trafford though is not one he remembers with any great fondness:

> I scored my one and only own goal. I was back on my own eighteen yard line – not sure what I was doing back there – and I put it back to the goalkeeper, and lobbed him, straight into my own net! It would have been great at the other end – the perfect own goal.

The highlight of Don's time with England youth came in the late spring of 1964 when he took part in an international tournament in Rotterdam. By now he was an established regular in Swindon's Second Division side, and he felt this experience stood him in good stead.

> I think the standard would definitely be on a par with the Second Division at least. We had a really good side, and that was shown by the number of players who went on and played in the First Division. Look at them – Harry Redknapp played wide on the right, with Peter Knowles, who left the game because he wanted to follow religion (Jehovah's Witnesses), inside him. David Sadler was centre forward, John Sissons was inside left and I was outside left. The two full-backs were Mick Wright, who played for Aston Villa's first team, and Bobby Noble who played for Manchester United but had a very bad accident. Howard Kendall played – he was the captain, and Peter Springett was in goal; John Hollins played, and so did Alf Wood from Manchester City. Three years on you looked at that squad when they were all playing in the First Division and thought – no wonder we did so well!

The tournament was a huge success, both for England, and for Don. He played in all the games, and scored in the group game against the Republic of Ireland, the semi-final against Portugal, and then twice in the 4-0 win over Spain in the final of the competition. For his efforts, he was voted the outstanding player in the tournament:

> My memory of the tournament isn't that great to be honest – all I can remember is scoring two goals in the final. They gave me a statuette for those goals, which I broke on the way home and had to have repaired! It was a pleasure to play in that team though: everyone was so good, and it was a very strong team.

For the record, the team that played in the final with Don was: Springett (Queens Park Rangers), M. Wright (Aston Villa), Noble (Manchester United); Kendall (Preston North End, captain), B. Wright (Leeds United), Hollins (Chelsea); Redknapp (West Ham United), Knowles (Wolverhampton Wanderers), Sadler (Manchester United), Sissons (West Ham United), Rogers (Swindon Town). Some familiar names there, although none would go on to be regular England internationals.

The next step up was the Under-23 side. Although the maximum age group for this team was reduced a few years back (hence it is now the England Under-21s), it remains a good opportunity for the England management team to look at their most promising talent, with a view to deciding who might make the step up to the full international side. Nowadays, the under-21s have their own management team. Back then it was a bit different: 'I was very surprised by the call-up. I found out because *The Advertiser* told me I'd been called up – there was no formal notification back then.'

Don being called up for the Under-23s was a remarkable achievement. He was, lest we forget, playing in the Third Division, and with the call up being in 1965, was just twenty-one. Don, therefore, joins a select band of players who have represented their country, at any level, while playing for a club side outside the top two divisions. Don's most famous predecessor at Swindon, Harold Fleming, did play at full international level for England while the club were still non-League, but that was a vastly different era to Don's.

> It was very hard to play in a game like that, because I didn't know anyone, other than Ernie Hunt, who also played. I can see why they say that teams need to be together for a week to get to know each other. I think I may even have gone the same day, so it wasn't ideal. It was also odd coming from a different division to most of the other players – unless you're very outgoing, which I wasn't.

England won the game, which was played at Southampton's (then) home ground, The Dell, on 24 November 1965, Martin Chivers scoring the winner eleven minutes from time after Yugoslavia had equalised an earlier goal by Mick Jones. The England team was: Stepney (Millwall); Lawler (Liverpool), Thomson (Wolverhampton Wanderers); Hollins (Chelsea), Mobley (Sheffield Wednesday), T. Smith (Liverpool); Armstrong (Arsenal), Hunt (Wolverhampton Wanderers), Jones (Sheffield United), Chivers (Southampton), Rogers (Swindon Town).

The whole Swindon Town team went down to cheer him on, including Keith Morgan: 'I sat next to John Charles – The Gentle Giant – at Southampton, and he turned to me in the second half and said "that Don Rogers is a good player isn't he?" He didn't know who I was, he was just commenting on what he was watching.'

Don was to play once more for the Under-23s, against Wales, in a game that England won 2-1, on 1 November 1967.

> The thing I remember most about the Welsh game was the fact that it rained all day. In fact, driving down to Swansea, I wondered whether the game would still be on. You had to treat the games as a one-off though and just do your best.

Originally, the many Swindon fans who made the trip west were hoping to see two Swindon players, as Rod Thomas had been selected for the Welsh side. It would have been doubly interesting, because as a right full-back, Thomas would have been in direct opposition to his colleague on the England left wing. Don diplomatically notes that, had Thomas played, 'honours would have been even, as Rod was just as quick as me'. In the event, Thomas was a late withdrawal due to injury.

ENGLAND JUST HOME IN FARCICAL CONDITIONS – SPIRITED FIGHT BY WALES

by Roger Malone
(The Daily Telegraph)

Wales Under-23 1 England under-23 2

England, so superior on paper, found a mixture of Welsh spirit, mud and swirling rain an impossible basis for sustained skill, and had to be content with a narrow win at Swansea last night. England scored a good goal after nine minutes and a brave winner thirteen minutes from time. In between, a young Fourth Division reserve, Geoff Thomas, grabbed himself a rare slice of glory by equalising with a strong fifteen-yard shot.

Conditions were always difficult, and for the last half-hour quite farcical for first-class football. During this last phase, as both teams looked for the winning goal, the pitch was a sea of mud and water in a twenty-yard strip down the middle.

Players could not break fast with the ball because to do so would mean the ball was left behind as it stuck in the mud. Numbers on players' backs were invisible because everyone was covered in mud.

Peter Osgood and Donald Rogers stood out as the game's two most dangerous raiders, particularly in the first twenty minutes. Osgood struck home a fine volley from Hollins' clever, low free-kick, to put England in front. Rogers showed powerful running and scored the winner from close range when Osgood nodded the ball on to him.

Thomas' equaliser was on the hour, and, seven minutes from time, David Payne, of Crystal Palace, replacing the injured Birchenall, made an unpleasant international debut – very short, very wet. Kidd and Lewis were booked after 40 minutes following a mild scrimmage.

Wales Under-23: Walker (York City); Coldrick (Cardiff City), Collins (Tottenham Hotspur); Powell (Wrexham), Mielczarek (Huddersfield Town), G. Thomas (Swansea); B. Lewis (Cardiff City), Hawkins (Leeds United), John Roberts (Swansea), W. Jones (Bristol Rovers), Walley (Watford).

England Under-23: Clemence (Liverpool); Badger (Sheffield United), Hughes (Liverpool); Kendall (Everton), Sadler (Manchester United), Hollins (Chelsea); Rogers (Swindon Town), Knowles (Wolverhampton Wanderers), Osgood (Chelsea), Birchenall (Sheffield United), Kidd (Manchester United). Subsitutue: Payne (Crystal Palace)

The *Evening Advertiser*'s Clive King was also in attendance, but was less than glowing in his report writing.

> Generally, however, the Swindon winger's performance was not one of his best, in conditions which obviously did not suit his style of play. Although he showed that he had the necessary class for this type of football, Rogers failed to supplement his good use of the ball, control and speed with the urgency required for the big occasion. He tended to be left out by not producing as large an appetite for possession as that shown by his colleagues.

Nothing like supporting your own man…

It is interesting to see that five of the victorious England youth team of 1964 had graduated to the next level, although by this stage David Sadler had converted from centre forward to centre half. Interesting also to note the date of the game, November 1967, the month Don submitted a transfer request to Swindon. It is probable, and Don does not deny it now, that playing with First Division players at international level accentuated his desire to play on a regular basis in top-flight football.

By October 1968, Don's international career was over. Too old now for the Under-23s (at a time when the playing of 'over-age' players was not allowed — thankfully why it was ever permitted is beyond me), his only hope of furthering his international career was to reach the full England side. To do that he would have to overcome two huge obstacles — the fact that he was playing outside the top level of English football, and the fact that his national manager, Sir Alf Ramsey, was not exactly famous for his love of wingers. In truth, Don was more focused on his club: 'Things were going really well at Swindon at that time, and to be honest, playing internationally was the last thing on my mind. I know it sounds like the right thing to say, but it's the truth!'

John Trollope feels his colleague would have done a good job at full international level:

> I think Don should have played for England, but he was unlucky in that at that time, Sir Alf Ramsay didn't want wingers, he wanted workmanlike midfielders. People like Don, and others such as Terry Paine and Peter Thompson, were very unfortunate really, because they were good enough to have played.

Don wasn't forgotten though:

> I got a couple of Christmas cards from Sir Alf, which I've kept — I thought it was worth it, even though I've given most of my other stuff away. He was very quiet, Sir Alf, very well spoken too — not like a football manager — but he got results. The problem for me of course was that he changed the whole nature of football by not picking wingers.

There was to be one further representative honour bestowed on Don by Sir Alf. It came during the 1969/70 season, Swindon's first back in the Second Division, when Don was called up for the annual match between the Football League and the Scottish League. These matches are now long since consigned to history, but at that stage they were treated reasonably seriously by both parties, with Sir Alf Ramsey himself picking the Football League side.

It came at a time when there was a concerted campaign by some members of the press, and some influential people in football, to try and get Don a place in the squad for the 1970 World Cup finals in Mexico. The ITV experts included Don in their All-Star squad that would 'beat the world'. This was a Great Britain side, and the team makes interesting reading – further evidence of how highly Don was rated by some. The full team was: Gordon Banks, Keith Newton, Mike England, Bobby Moore, Terry Cooper, Alan Ball, Billy Bremner, Francis Lee, Jimmy Greaves, Ron Davies and George Best, with Don as substitute.

Further evidence of how well regarded Don was came when the FA secretary, Dennis Follows, spoke at a dinner in Swindon, and commented 'If I had anything to do with the choosing of the England team, he would be with us next year in Mexico.'

Don wasn't to make the squad, but at least he did get some recognition by being picked for the game against the Scots, as he recalls:

> It was a great honour, given the rest of the team. I think I was drafted in when Peter Thompson dropped out, and it was the closest I ever came to playing for England really, especially when you look at who else played.

The 1970 match took place at Highfield Road, Coventry, on 18 March 1970, and the Football League lined up like this: Stepney (Manchester United); Smith (Sheffield Wednesday), Hughes (Liverpool); Newton (Everton), McFarland (Derby County), Todd (Derby County); Coates (Burnley), Kidd (Manchester United),

Astle (West Bromwich Albion), Harvey (Everton), Rogers (Swindon Town). Subs: Glazier (Coventry City), Peters (Tottenham). Spot the odd men out? It's Don and the Sheffield Wednesday full-back, Smith. All the others in the starting eleven would make at least one appearance for the full England side.

In the event, England won 3-2, with two goals from Jeff Astle and one from Don himself. What does he recall about the game? 'I remember the goal – a shot from eighteen yards – the winner. I really enjoyed it, although it was difficult initially because you don't know anyone and they all know each other from playing in the First Division.'

He was supported by at least one loyal fan from Swindon, Clive Bettison: 'I got in from work at five o'clock, picked up the paper and saw that Don had been called up to play, so on the spur of the moment I decided to go up to Coventry to go and see him. It was a difficult journey back then, without motorways, but I got there just after kick-off, and well in time to see Don score.'

DON ROGERS PLAYS A LEADING ROLE

by Clive King
(*Evening Advertiser*)

Don Rogers, the Swindon Town left-winger had a night of glory when he helped the Football League defeat the Scottish League by 3-2 at Coventry last night.

Rogers, a late replacement for Peter Thompson, started the move which led to the first goal and then banged in a splendid second goal as the League side cruised to a comfortable lead.

Rogers would have had a second goal but for a fearless save by McRae, and his form brought envious glances from the array of managers and scouts at the game. The only Second Division player in the side, Rogers started the move which led to the first goal after 16 minutes. He cut inside and, when Greig challenged, found Kidd with a pin-point pass on the left. The

Manchester United man centred perfectly for Astle to head home.

Eight minutes later, McKinnon beat Astle in the air to a centre from Coates, but he could not clear. Rogers chested the ball down, controlled it, and then slammed it home for a great goal.

In the second half the Scots came more into the game. Cormack pulled one back, but Astle again restored the two-goal lead. Graham made it 3-2 fifteen minutes from time.

Football League: – (as above on previous page)

Scottish League: MacRae (Motherwell); Callaghan (Dunfermline), Dickson (Kilmarnock); Smith (Rangers), McKinnon (Rangers), Stanton (Hibernian); McLean (Kilmarnock), Greig (Rangers), Hall (St Johnstone). Subs: Graham (Hibernian), Cormack (Hibernian), Johnston (Rangers).

Don would eventually reach the top flight when he moved to Crystal Palace, but he was twenty-seven by the time he made his First Division debut. Despite the phenomenal impact he made early on at Palace, with Ramsey still in charge, and England fighting to qualify for the 1974 World Cup (they didn't make it), an international call-up was always unlikely, although after Palace beat Southampton 2-0 at Selhurst Park in the FA Cup in January 1973, and Ted Bates made his famous quote of 'Don Rogers is the best player in the country at the moment' he came close –as the chapter on his time at Palace makes clear. In an era where players of the talent of Peter Osgood, Alan Hudson and Frank Worthington won but a handful of caps, Don, as another flair player, was to miss out. As he said earlier in the book, in his mind, it was the closest he ever came…

The London papers did their best to be honest. They gave me some great write-ups and led a campaign for me to be picked. If I was going to have played for England then it would have been then. I had a really good start at Palace and things went so well that I was probably a bit unlucky not to have got picked. Part of it though was that Alf Ramsey was still the manager and he didn't really like flair players – he wanted grafters – they could play mind, but they were very hard workers.

Alan Whittle, like Don, an England Under-23 international, believes that Ramsey was too cautious in his approach to new players: 'The international scene was a bit of a closed shop really. Like Don, I was waiting for a full international call-up, and it never came, mainly because Sir Alf kept picking the same players; I guess you could say he was very loyal, but at the time it was very frustrating. What made it worse was that after Sir Alf went, it seemed like everybody got given a cap – many of whom weren't fit to lace Don's boots.'

So, had Don moved earlier from Swindon, would he have played for his country? What if that bid from Liverpool in 1965 had been accepted? Certainly those who saw Don at his peak in the First Division with Palace have no doubt. Peter Gee simply states: 'How he never played for England is a mystery'. Keith Morgan agrees: 'It's terrible that he never played for England as a full international when you consider some of the people who have been capped. I know Ramsey didn't like wingers, but you would have thought he would have tried Don out.'

Frank Burrows thinks that had Don left Swindon earlier, he would have been called up: 'He undoubtedly should have played for England. If you look at what happened when he finally left Swindon, he made such an impact at Palace that he must have come close to having getting picked. Just imagine what he would have been like had he left earlier in his career. I'm sure he would have been picked. He was so comfortable at Palace, and at the First Division level, it's where he should have played.'

Finally, from among his teammates, Rod Thomas. Thomas, as somebody who played over fifty times for his country, is perhaps best placed to make a judgement. 'He was international class, no doubt about it. Some of the players who have played since… well it's a joke really when you consider that Don never got a cap. When I went to Derby I played in a Championship-winning team with twelve or so internationals on the books, all good players, but if I were composing a side based on the teammates I had in my playing career, Don would be one of my first choices.'

As for Don, it is the one time in our conversations when he looks more than a little wistful:

> I would have loved to played one game. Most people think that I did play for England, but I didn't quite make it unfortunately. Mind you, I wasn't the only one to miss out – a lot of good players didn't get picked.

Here then is another of our 'what ifs'. Don was very close – there is no doubt about that – but was hampered by circumstance. Don was at his peak in 1972/73, Ramsey at that stage was in his final year as the national manager. His temporary replacement was Joe Mercer who, along with Malcolm Allison, had tried to sign Don for Manchester City. By the spring of 1974 though, when Mercer took charge, Don was back in the First Division with Palace. Had Mercer been appointed a year previously, when Don was the talk of the top flight, it doesn't seem too far-fetched to say that he would have given Don a game, in the same way that he gave caps to players such as Frank Worthington and Keith Weller. Once again, if only…

An Unhappy Ranger

At first glance, the move to QPR looked an ideal move for Don. He was able to stay in London and he joined a side that, under manager Gordon Jago, were seeking to establish themselves in the First Division. In a way, Rangers were a similar type of club to Palace – not one of London's traditional giants, but a club for whom playing in the top flight was a relatively new experience. Like Swindon, Rangers had achieved the 'double' of promotion from the Third Division and the League Cup, and this success, in 1967, was followed by a first-ever promotion to the First Division a year later. Relegation was immediate after a disastrous first season in the top flight, but they were promoted again in 1973, and had finished a very creditable eighth in their first season back at the top level.

What was more, they seemed to want play the type of football that Don would enjoy. They had another talented winger in the shape of England Under-23 star Dave Thomas, and the midfield ability of future England captain Gerry Francis, not to mention the mercurial Stan Bowles. Up front, the Republic of Ireland striker Don Givens was a prolific scorer.

Despite all this talent, Don joined a club in a position that had become all too familiar to him – near the bottom. Rangers had only won one of their first eight games (remarkably, away at

Champions Leeds United, although this was during Brian Clough's ill-fated reign at Elland Road). With just five points, they were in twentieth position.

Don's first game for Rangers was in a midweek home match against Everton at Loftus Road. He came off the bench to help Rangers secure a 2-2 draw, their first point for four games. Three days later, his career at Rangers, after just thirteen days at the club took a major change for the worse when Gordon Jago resigned.

Even now, thirty years later, it is not completely clear what happened. At the time, the chairman, Jim Gregory, said that Jago had resigned and that the board had accepted his decision. Two days later, Jago gave an interview where he said he resigned because he was demoted to team manager only, and was not going to be allowed 'to do the job for which I have been appointed'. Whatever the actual events, it was clear that all was not well at Loftus Road. There had been much talk about unrest within the club. Venables, as one of the most influential members of the dressing room, had been sold, experienced centre half Terry Mancini had been trans-fer-listed, and Stan Bowles had been suspended for two weeks for failing to attend training. What was Don's take on it all?

> The dressing-room seemed alright when I arrived, although it was very clear that there were some strong characters around – especially people like Stan Bowles. It was a huge shock when Gordon Jago left. I'd only just arrived, and I remember thinking 'What's going on here?' I also realised very quickly how influen-tial the chairman was – he really ran the club and could do anything at anytime – although he always liked to be one of the boys.

Without a manager, and with coach Stan Anderson in temporary charge, Rangers travelled north to play Manchester City on 28 September. A 1-0 defeat, with Don again on the bench, this time coming on for Don Givens, left Rangers bottom of the First Division. Did Don wonder what he had done?

I didn't really worry too much about what was happening, because
I could see that we had a good side; with all respect to Palace, it was
a better all-round team and I thought we would improve. Also, I
was just happy to be playing back in the First Division, so I wasn't
going to let a couple of defeats concern me too much.

Don was substitute again when Rangers won only their second
game of the season by beating Ipswich 1-0 at Loftus Road. A
welcome win for his side, although the win was somewhat overshadowed by the antics of Irish centre half Terry Mancini, who
pulled his shorts down in what he called a 'gesture of jubilation' in
front of the directors box. Unsurprisingly, he never played for
Rangers again.

I ask Don about this incident, certain that Don will give me a
good story about what happened. Sadly though, he doesn't have a
clear memory of the events at the final whistle…

Don made his first start in a blue-and-white hoped shirt when he
played at Arsenal on 12 October – Rangers gaining another point in
a creditable 2-2 draw. However, as Don sought to establish himself, a
new man was en route, Dave Sexton, who was appointed manager
on 16 October. It was an appointment that Don welcomed:

It seemed like a great appointment for me, because he had tried to
sign me eighteen months earlier when I was at Palace and he was
at Chelsea, so I thought he must rate me. You always wonder what
will happen when the manager changes, but this time I looked to
have landed on my feet.

Sexton joined two weeks after parting company with Chelsea, where
he had enjoyed huge success, leading them to both FA and European
Cup Winners Cup glory at the start of the 1970s. The more recent
past though had seen Chelsea struggle, however, and Sexton was
asked to leave by the Chelsea chairman Brian Mears. Rangers saw
their chance to get an experienced First Division manager and
Sexton was on his way from one West London club to another.

History will judge Dave Sexton as a reasonably successful manager. His time at QPR was to coincide with the best season in the club's history – the 1975/76 runners-up position in the First Division, and he would then move on to one of the top (although at that time, probably not the top) managerial roles in the country when he succeeded Tommy Docherty as manager of Manchester United in the summer of 1977. He would later coach at international level with England.

Initially, little appeared to change for Don. He started Sexton's first game in charge, a 1-0 home defeat to Liverpool, and also the next two games, both of which were won, to move Rangers up to the dizzy heights of sixteenth in the table. However, he had to adjust to a new position:

> As soon as he came in, Sexton said to me that he wanted me to play in central midfield and use my passing ability there. It was a bit difficult to adjust really after fifteen years playing wide – it sounds daft to say it, but you don't know where to make your runs half of the time. I enjoyed it, but it didn't last very long – only a couple of games or so.

Don missed the next game, a 5-2 defeat at eventual Champions Derby County, but played in the next four games, scoring his first goal for the club in a 3-1 win at Middlesbrough on 23 November.'

> I was very pleased with the goal at Middlesbrough. It's always important to score your first goal for a new club, and I was back playing wide then. I got the ball on the edge of the box, beat the full-back and then put it past the 'keeper.

Don was now starting to adjust to playing with his new teammates:

> They were a really good set of players; if you look back now they were nearly all internationals, and all capable of doing something

special. Quite why we had been struggling I don't know, because there was a lot of talent in the team. It was a good team for me to play in though because we all wanted to play football the way it should be played – ball to feet – and that suited me.

After missing another game, Don scored another goal, this time the winner in the 1-0 win over Sheffield United at Loftus Road, although the crowd, just over 13,000, was an indication that Rangers fans were not yet completely sure of the Sexton revival. It was certainly a change from Palace

> Rangers certainly weren't as big a club as Palace in terms of facilities or fans, although their supporters were just as fanatical. It was a good place to play football but it was a bit different because the whole ground was much smaller than Palace's.

Rangers were now seventeenth and Sexton was slowly starting to have an impact. At the back, the experienced pairing of Dave Webb and Frank McLintock were tightening up the defence, Don Givens was scoring goals up front, and Gerry Francis was the midfield general. Yet all was not quite right in the Rangers camp: on 7 December, Stan Bowles was put on the transfer list – for thirty days only, and with the agreement that if nobody came forward to meet the £250,000 asking price (which would be a British record) then Bowles would stay at the London club. In fact Bowles was to stay on the transfer list for just ten days, before withdrawing his request. It was the third time that year that Bowles had been on the list.

> Stan Bowles was a superb player, absolutely superb. He was one of the first players I saw who used to hand players off and get away with it. When he knew he was going to get the ball, he used to just push the defender away with his hand, so when he got the ball he had that extra bit of space. He used to get lots of kicks though because everyone wanted to stop him; he eventually took to playing with wads of cotton wool around his ankles!

Don had now started in eight of Sexton's first ten matches, playing as a both a central midfielder, and in his more traditional wide position. However, after that appearance, in the middle of December, he would start just four of the last twenty League games of the season. What happened?

> I just lost form really – the injury was starting to take effect and I was rapidly losing my pace, which made it more difficult, especially when I was playing wide or up front. The experiment of playing me in midfield was short-lived, and Sexton brought Don Masson in to play in that position, so my opportunity there wasn't likely to be that great going forward.

After two months out of the first team, Don returned, as substitute for the FA Cup fifth-round tie at West Ham on 15 February. The Hammers had beaten Swindon after a replay in the fourth round, and proved too strong, winning by 2-1 en route to an eventual FA Cup final victory over Fulham. Don came on for Stan Bowles, who launched another assault on Sexton after being substituted. 'I'll never talk to him again' is what he was reported as saying after the match. Things were soon patched up though, as was another row, this time between Sexton and Dave Webb. Don plays it all down: 'The dressing room had very strong people in it, and when you've got that you are always going to get things said in the heat of the moment. I wouldn't call it an unhappy dressing-room though; just one where people spoke their mind!'

Don started the next game, a win at Carlisle, and then came off the bench, after another game out, to score the winner against Luton on 1 March. He was again missing the following week though, as the side lost at Everton, You will now be becoming familiar with a sense of stop-start about Don's Rangers career – in fact the longest run of successive games that Don had in a Rangers shirt was four – which was very frustrating for somebody who had been a virtual ever-present at Swindon and Palace.

It was horrible because you're in and out of the team all of the time and it becomes hard to know where you stand. You then find it harder to motivate yourself, and you're wondering all the time how you are doing, whereas if you are playing every week you know things are all right and even if you have a bad game, which everybody does, you'll be picked the following week. From my own personal position, I needed to be playing every week, given my age.

We were now in mid-March, but for Don the season had just four games to go, one as substitute. He scored twice in the 2-0 home win over Manchester City at Loftus Road on 15 March 1975, and also played in the 1-0 home win over Sexton's old club, Chelsea, three days later. He obviously did something wrong, because he was dropped for the trip to Birmingham four days later where Rangers lost 4-1.

I missed a sitter against Chelsea, which probably led to me losing my place. I tried to be too clever – it was a volley from about six yards, which I thought I'd place into the top of the net, but I put it over the bar. I should have just shut my eyes and put it in the net. I missed a couple that night.

The Manchester City game was my best one for QPR. I scored two good goals that day: one was a half-volley from about eighteen yards, and the other was a through ball down the middle which I took and went round the goalkeeper.

There is no tape of the Manchester City game that I have been able to discover. However, listening to Don's description, one thing is clear: the solo goal he scored that day was the last trademark Rogers goal – running through the centre of a defence, and beating the 'keeper one-on-one.

Don's final game of the season was the home game against Spurs on 29 March, Easter Saturday. Rangers lost 1-0, and Don finished his first season at Loftus Road with the record of 5 goals from 13 full League appearances plus five as substitute – not a bad record at all. However, although he didn't know it at the time, the Spurs game was not only his final game of the season, it was his final ever game for Rangers. 'We had done well in the second half of the season, although from a personal viewpoint it had been difficult because I hadn't been playing regularly. I was pleased with my scoring record, but I knew I would find it difficult to get into the first team, if everybody was fit.'

As we have already seen, season 1975/76 was a memorable one for Queens Park Rangers Football Club. Had Wolves not conceded three second-half goals in their final match at home to Liverpool, then Rangers would have been Champions. It was a tremendous achievement by the West London club, which, as now, lacked the resources to compete financially with some of their bigger London rivals. Key to their success was a consistent team selection – they only used seventeen players all season, and of those players five made just fourteen appearances between them. By contrast, six players – goalkeeper Phil Parkes, right-back Dave Clement, left-back Ian Gillard, winger Dave Thomas, midfielder Don Masson, and centre forward Don Givens – each played over 40 games. It was a very settled and successful side (the two usually go together) and Don couldn't force his way in: 'It was the best side I was ever involved with. Lots of great players, and some of the football was an absolute joy to watch. It was a great shame that they didn't win the League. I doubt a club of that size will get that close again.'

Back in 1975/76, football was a little different. This was still the days of one substitute, not five. While some of those Rangers players would have been feeling tired towards the end of the season, 'squad rotation' was not a phrase in Dave Sexton (or indeed any other manager's) armoury. Don therefore was not involved in the first team at all, not even via a regular seat on the bench. Instead his Saturday afternoons would be spent playing in the football graveyard that was the Football Combination.

Nowadays reserve-team matches can be played anywhere, at any time. Many Premiership clubs do not use their own grounds for reserve-team games – preferring instead to save their pitches and to play at local non-League grounds. In 1975 this wasn't the case. Reserve-team fixtures took place on a Saturday afternoon, in front of very small crowds, who focused less on the football in front of them than on the latest news of the first team, playing away in some far-flung part of the country. It was a place for youngsters learning their trade, and a few hardened, experienced pros, winding down their careers. At twenty-nine, Don fitted into neither category.

> I can't pretend it wasn't very difficult because I had never had a period in my career when I hadn't been a first-team regular. You just have to do your best though, and one of the things I'm most proud of is a comment by Frank Sibley, the Rangers reserve team manager, after a game at Plymouth. He said in front of the whole dressing room after the game that it was a great pleasure to see someone like Don Rogers putting 100 per cent into a reserve team game, and if the young lads in the team had the same attitude throughout their career, they would be all right.

Playing in the reserves can be a desperate experience. Eamon Dunphy, in his best-selling book about the life of a professional footballer in the mid-1970s , *Only a Game?*, describes it thus:

> There is no-one there, absolutely nothing at stake, except your own pride. You don't feel like it at all. And whereas for two hours before a first-team game you are beginning to feel nervous, beginning to get geed up, feeling a bit of tension and atmosphere, here you go to a ground which is empty. It is like a graveyard.

There seemed no way out. Don couldn't force his way into the first team, and there seemed to be no clubs interested in rescuing him from his nightmare. Instead he turned out, week in, week out, for Rangers reserves. It would be good to record that, at very least, he inspired them to a memorable Championship win, but alas, he couldn't. Over the season, Rangers reserves finished an uninspiring twelfth.

You realise that with the first team doing so well, that you've got no real chance of being selected, no matter how well you play, and it makes the games very hard. Dave Sexton, to be fair, was good to me. He kept coming over and seeing me during training, because I was still training with the first team, and telling me to 'keep going.'

With hindsight, I went there a couple of years too late. Had I been fitter and on top form I think it would have worked very well, because the way they played football suited me, and I would have fitted in very well.

At both Crystal Palace and Swindon, Don remains a major hero. At Rangers, few can remember him. There is virtually no media coverage of his time at Loftus Road, and the official history of Queens Park Rangers doesn't mention him at all. It is as if his time there never existed; a huge contrast to the memories that exist from his time at his other two clubs. He is probably right when he says that he went there too late – had he gone there at the peak of his career, it would have been a different story.

Then, in early March, a lifeline. A club wanted to sign Don. Would he be interested? It probably wouldn't have mattered who it was, he would have been. In fact, it was his old club – the Robins of Swindon.

I knew that Danny Williams had come to watch me play for the reserves, so when I got the call to say I could go back to Swindon I was delighted. I needed a change, and of course going back to Swindon was ideal, particularly for the family, because we'd always said that we would end up back in Swindon to live. On and off the pitch it seemed the right thing.

On 5 March 1976, Don re-signed for Swindon for £30,000. The local hero was back.

Return of the Hero

Before looking at Don's second spell at Swindon, it's worth catching up with events at the County Ground in his absence, so we can put his return into some sort of context. As we have seen, Swindon were relegated to the Third Division, along with Palace, at the end of the 1973/74 season, having had a disastrous campaign and only accumulating 25 points, which, even under the old two-points-for-a-win scenario, was an awful total. The poor results had led to a change in manager during the season. It was Don's old boss, Danny Williams, who took over from Les Allen in March, but the team were already too far adrift.

1974/75 saw a slow start. The team only won one of their first five matches, including the match which was the last time we encountered the Robins, the 6-2 defeat at Selhurst Park – Don's last game for Palace. However, the side gradually improved, and made a genuine push for promotion before finishing fourth. There was also an excellent cup run, which was only ended by eventual winners West Ham, in front of almost 27,000 people in a replay at the County Ground. The side was boosted by the goals of former Wolves reserve striker Peter Eastoe, who scored 31 in League and cup, and those of Witney-born winger David Moss, who scored 16.

After the near miss of 1974/75, there was a real expectation in the town that 1975/76 would be Swindon's year. It wasn't to be though. The side won only five League matches before Christmas and, despite an apparent revival early in the New Year, when they won four games in five, including a 6-3 victory over Aldershot at the County Ground, they then lost five out of the next six games, to mean that when Don arrived they were in twenty-second place and staring at the possibility of a first ever season in the Fourth Division.

John Trollope doesn't recall the time with any great fondness: 'It was the worst part of my career. We had so many good players replaced by lesser players, and I think Danny really struggled because he didn't have the quality of players that he had before and couldn't get them to blend together.'

Don had been away from the County Ground for nearly three-and-a-half years. Inevitably, in that time the team had changed hugely. From the team that played in his last game for Town in October 1972, only Frank Burrows and John Trollope remained, although Joe Butler – who missed Don's last game, but was a regular in that 1972/73 season – would make his final appearance for the club in Don's first game back.

It was, as Don would discover, a very different club from what he had left:

> It rarely works in football, going back. It's not the sort of thing you should do, and it was a different club altogether. I don't mean to be unkind, but the players there were nowhere near as good as the players I'd played with when I was there before, although, mind you, I wasn't as good either of course. It brings back bad memories now thinking about it – it can never be the same as it was.

Nearly thirty years on, it is difficult to convey the impact of Don's return to Swindon. It was the return of the prodigal son, albeit one who had left with everybody's best wishes, as John Trollope recalls:

Everybody thought that Don would spark us off again, and we would see the same old Don. What we didn't know was that he had severe injury problems; we knew he had injuries but didn't know how serious they were.

Frank Burrows felt sorry for Don: 'It was soon evident that it wasn't the Don I knew. He could still cross a ball and hit a mean shot, but the pace, the freedom of movement had gone. At that stage I was doing my coaching badges, and when I watched Don train, I could soon see that there was a problem, just by watching him move.'

The *Evening Advertiser* made Don's return to the club front-page news. It was a massive psychological boost for a team sorely in need of one.

Don recalls the response to his return fondly: 'It was lovely coming back, it really was. People were so pleased to see me. The problem was that everyone had really high expectations of me – 25 goals a season and all that, but it just couldn't happen.'

Don's first game back was a Tuesday evening game at home to Rotherham United. Rotherham were mid-table and unlikely to bring many fans south for a 7.30 p.m. kick-off. Swindon's previous home game, against Southend United, had attracted a gate of 5,587. The Don factor though, meant that the attendance for the Rotherham game was nearly 10,000. They were all there to see one man, and he didn't disappoint, although it's not a particularly good memory for him: 'It wasn't a very good game, and I can remember wondering what I had come back to. Even the goal wasn't very good – the goalkeeper should have saved it – and at the end of the game I realised just how hard it was going to be.'

(As a totally frivolous aside, I had always believed that the Rotherham goal had been scored by a man whose name gave me much childish amusement: Trevor Womble. Sadly, my research for this book showed that it was scored by the much more anonymously-named Jimmy Goodfellow. Another childhood myth exposed...)

Don played in the next match, a 2-0 win in the unglamorous surroundings of The Shay at Halifax, in front of under 2,000 spectators, but although he started in each of the next two games, away at Brighton and at home to Mansfield, both were lost, and he was substituted in both, as he sought to get his fitness back. 'It was very tough, because I wasn't fully fit and hadn't been for a long time, so I had to play in a different way. I wasn't the same speedy winger that everyone remembered.'

Swindon's position, despite the boost of Don's return, was now critical. They were bottom of the table, with just nine games of the season to go. Don missed the next game, a midweek home win against Chester, but was back for a 4-0 thumping at Chesterfield on 3 April, a result which left the Robins in twenty-third place. Yet from somewhere, with Don mainly wearing an unfamiliar number four shirt, they went on a run that would save them – three successive victories. The most crucial of these was a 1-0 win at relegation rivals Aldershot. Had the game been drawn, and all other results unchanged, then Swindon, not Aldershot, would have been relegated.

Despite that run, however, they still were not safe. Four games to go, and the next two were tricky: an away match at Cardiff, and a home game against Millwall. Both of these teams were going for promotion (and would ultimately be successful in their efforts). Swindon took one point from those two games – a 0-0 draw at Cardiff before the 2-0 home defeat by Millwall. The latter game was Don's final action of the season, as he limped off.

In the event, Swindon, without Don, survived. A 5-1 home win over Walsall on 24 April was crucial. It featured the unusual occurrence of a hat-trick of penalties, all taken, and scored by, the Irish international Trevor Anderson. A 2-2 draw against Wrexham at the County Ground five days later confirmed safety. It had been very close.

John Trollope: 'I think Don found it very difficult coming bac ,into the side. It wasn't the best of periods for the club, and Don wasn't the player he was. You could just see that the movement wasn't the same as it been – that ability to float had gone.'

Don himself doesn't have happy memories either. 'It wasn't doing me any good at all. I was getting slower and slower because of the hip, without realising it most of the time. I just had no pace. It wasn't any fun and I wasn't enjoying it.'

Everyone connected with the club looked forward to an improved 1976/77. It would be a better year, with the team finishing mid-table in the Third Division and also embarking on a thrilling FA Cup run, that saw them score eight goals in two games against George Best's Fulham, and only succumb late on in a replay at Everton in the fourth round, after a 2-2 draw at the County Ground that will be best remembered for Kenny Stroud's 'goal of the season'.

For Don though, injury meant that time was running out. At just thirty, his fourteen-year career in professional football was coming to an end.

Don played just twice that season: in a 1-0 win at Chesterfield on 4 September, where he scored in the winner, and then, his final game in League football, a 1-0 home win against Oxford United on 27 December.

'I went on loan to play for Yeovil in the autumn, because Stan Harland was player-manager there and I was asked to help him out. I really wasn't fit enough to play League football, which is why I barely played that season. In fact I didn't play many games at Yeovil either. You've got to remember that my first hip replacement was early 1979, and it was hurting pretty much all the time for eighteen months before that.

After a total of 500 League appearances and 181 goals, it was over.

I should never have come back to Swindon really. It was definitely a mistake. People expected far too much – they thought it would be like it was in the good old days. I did feel the pressure, because I knew I wasn't the same player, and that the players round me weren't the same. I was getting slower and slower and wasn't fit enough to make the contribution I would have liked, even at Third Division level.

Life After Football

Aged thirty-two, Don was now forced to look elsewhere for a living. His fourteen-year career as a professional footballer was now over.

For many footballers, life after football is a difficult time. Few have planned what they will do, or have much in the way of qualifications to fall back on. With limited opportunities to continue in football via management or coaching, historically it has been running a pub or selling something (traditionally financial services) that has been the career of choice. For Don, things were different. He had a ready-made career to fall back on; moreover, one that he had been actively following since 1968 as he was owner of a sports shop (although *The Football League Review* reported in 1969 that Don had also considered 'starting a driving school or opening a wallpaper shop' before settling on his new business venture).

> I opened the shop with Derek May, who in fact was a scout for Wolves, and somebody I knew well from playing table tennis. 1968 was a great time to open the shop – just before we got to Wembley – and business was excellent. I used to go down there most afternoons and help out, and of course people wanted to come in and chat about football to me, which was great.

Looking back on it we really didn't know what we were doing. We seemed to spend most of our time ordering football boots, because we only used to order one set of boots at a time, and they soon went! I remember that Adidas, which was the main boot at the time – you had to stock Adidas – wouldn't supply us at first, because they were a bit careful about who they gave their stock to, so we actually got the Adidas boots from Danny Williams' sports shop in Rotherham! They soon relented though when it was evident that we were going to be successful.

Soon there was another boot to stock: the Don Rogers boot, brought out by a firm in Bristol, shortly after the League Cup triumph. This particular item, as Don says with his usual modesty, 'did quite well'.

Back in 1968, things were very different: 'We used to serve the customers from behind the counter – there was no self service like you get today. Of course, it was a simpler business as well: we used to only stock six types of football shirts, whereas now it's about 160. We did well though, supplying kits and boots to football clubs, as well as individuals, and then later we went into dealing with local tennis clubs and table tennis clubs – both sports which I personally played.'

Overall, the shop has been a big success, although Don admits that there were things they could have done differently:

I sometimes think that we didn't make enough of the name that I had in the game, and that we could have been a bit more ambitious – we were offered one of the first shops in the Brunel Centre (a Swindon shopping centre, revolutionary when it was opened just after Don set up his shop), but we were frightened to take it because of the rent. We were going to open shops in other towns as well, but we never got round to it apart from one in Stroud which didn't go very well, and we had to close down. We should have gone for bigger towns really – a place like Bath was the sort of place we always talked about.

Nevertheless, the original shop has survived, and continues to thrive.

> We're doing better now than we've ever done. It's been all family now for a few years, which helps, because it means that if we say we're going to do something then we do it. The other thing is that I always give the best prices I can to people, and they know that – it doesn't matter if people are buying one thing or one hundred things, I'll do the best deal I can for people.
>
> One of the nice things for me is the number of people who still come in from all over the world, and want to talk about football – especially Wembley 1969. It was also great that for five or ten years after I left Palace people from London used to make the trip to Swindon to see me: they always knew where they could find me.

This has deliberately been a biography that focuses on Don's professional, rather than his private, life. This is the way that Don, a naturally private man, would prefer. However, now is probably the time to acknowledge the part played by his family: his wife, Jane, who he married at Christ church in Swindon in 1967, and his daughters, Emma, born in March 1972, and Lucy, born in April 1973.

> I've been very lucky in my family life. If you look at my parents, they did a huge amount for me. My dad was like me: he was very quiet and he didn't say much, although I'm sure he was very proud. Jane's parents have been almost like second parents down the years. I lived with them from 1964: I had to move out of the hostel because it was being redecorated, and as I was going out with Jane at the time, her parents invited me in... and I didn't leave until Jane and I got married.
>
> Jane and the girls have always been very supportive with what I've done, which is critical, because you can't do anything without that. I've now got four grandchildren as well – Josh, Ben, Amy and Jack. Three boys, so you never know, one of them might become a footballer, although I'd never push them into it. My two oldest

grandsons do like their football though, which is nice – the oldest one has only just got into it, but as keen as anything now.

So the shop thrives, and Don is quick to pay tribute to a good friend of his, the late Brian Bartlett, who 'did a huge amount for me and the shop' in the 1980s when times were tough. However, Don's other business venture, a building firm, also run initially with Derek May and started in the early 1970s, is no more. Don had to close it in 1991 because he couldn't get anyone to pay the money owing to him (some £60,000-£70,000).

Don's career was, of course, ended by injury. The surgeon who studied the X-rays of his left hip in 1974 was accurate when he suggested that a hip replacement would be needed in the not-too-distant future. The hip was duly replaced in early 1979, when Don was just thirty-three, and this was followed by further replacements in 1994 and 2004. Indeed, much of the work on this book was done as Don convalesced from his latest hip replacement in April 2004. Those of a squeamish disposition should skip the next bit… the hip was due to be replaced earlier in the year, but when they took the original hip out ready for replacement, they found an infection, so Don spent six weeks without any hip bone at all while they waited for it to clear – ouch!

I think that my first hip replacement would have lasted longer if I hadn't played football on it. I used to play for a Swindon Town Old Boys side (in fact called the Don Rogers XI, but Don is too modest to point this out). We had people like John Trollope, Terry Wollen, Wilf Tranter, Keith Morgan and Dave Moss playing. We even gave the old Swindon kit man, Eddie Buckley, the last ten minutes of games. It was great fun, but it didn't do the replacement hip any good – the surgeon couldn't believe it when I told him I'd be playing, and I don't think some of the opposition players believed it either, because for the first few years I was still quite quick.

In terms of involvement on the coaching and management side, Don's first role was back at his old club, as coach of the Swindon Town youth team from 1981 to 1983.

To put those years into historical perspective, sadly, they were some of the worst years in the club's history at first-team level. After they had come close to another League Cup final appearance in 1979/80, losing only to Wolves in the semi-finals, 1980/81 saw a poor start, culminating in the departure of manager Bobby Smith. His replacement was Don's old left-sided colleague, John Trollope. Although Trollope stabilised the side and kept them up in 1980/81, he was unable to prevent relegation to the Fourth Division in 1981/82, the side finally going down on a bleak night in Newport.

The next season, Swindon's first ever in the bottom rung of English football, started very well, with the side challenging for an immediate promotion at Christmas, but a run of poor results saw them fall away and cost Trollope his job. Ken Beamish took over, but also met with limited success. Crowds, which had been at the 20,000 level on a regular basis in Don's heyday, slipped below 2,000. Nevertheless, despite the problems elsewhere in the club, Don enjoyed his role:

> It was a very good two years. I fancied doing it, and when I was offered the job I didn't have to think too much about it. It wasn't a great side, but it was good fun. The star player at youth level was of course Paul Rideout, but I couldn't select him because he was playing for the first-team. He was different class – I was very surprised he didn't play for England. He was so strong for his age, a bit like Rooney now, I suppose.
>
> The team I inherited did well in my first year. Players like Ray Baverstock and Colin Baillie, who later played for the first team, were playing, and we won the Midland Youth Cup. It was a good side, but the later sides weren't in that class.
>
> I left at the end of the 1983 season, after Ken Beamish came in as manager – although I always got on very well with Ken, and we were friendly for years afterwards.

Don wasn't lost to the club for long though.

> From 1985 to 1989, I did the sponsors' lounge at Swindon. We did incredibly well, but the football, from a purist's viewpoint wasn't very good – some of the worst I've seen. From the crowd's view-point it was very exciting, and of course it was very successful, but I didn't enjoy watching it myself – in fact I used to go downstairs and miss half of the game, because I couldn't take it. Still, who am I to complain? The people in the sponsors' lounge were always happy and they were the ones paying for it.
>
> I remember the night we went up from the Fourth Division. I couldn't move in the lounge, I was pinned up against the bar. There were far too many people in there – goodness knows how it happened. It was packed.

Don was out of football for three years before a chance meeting changed the course of his life for the next decade.

> A bloke called Colin Moyle came into the shop one day to order some trophies. He was the manager of Lambourn. We got chatting and he asked me if I'd ever thought about getting involved with management. When I thought about it, I decided that, yes, I would quite like to have a go, so I met up with him and Clive Bettison – who I later discovered knew more about my career than I did myself! Anyway, they arranged for Jane and I to go out to Lambourn and, when I looked round, I thought that this was a really good little club and that I'd like to get involved.

At the time, July 1992, Don was quoted as saying 'I just wanted to do something in football again. Football was always my life, and still is really. Enjoyment is the main reason for taking on this position, so I'll give it a go. My approach to management is to play football – as simple as that. There won't be any of this long-ball stuff.'

Don looks back on his time in his first management job with real fondness:

I had four great years at Lambourn. We finished third or fourth in the first year, then third or fourth in the second year, but they promoted us because we were getting floodlights, so we went into the Hellenic Premier League. We had a great year in the first season at the top level. We finished third, and nearly got the runners-up spot. I remember we lost the first three games, and then won twelve out of the next fourteen. We also won the Berks & Bucks Cup at Maidenhead against Eton Wick. It was a great day out – we were a goal down at half time and beat them 2-1. I really enjoyed it – believe me, what matters is to win things, and it was just as good to win the Berks & Bucks Cup as it was to win at Wembley! Then, unfortunately, it all went sour and I left. One man, who shall remain nameless in this account, destroyed the club as far as I was concerned.

Clive Bettison confirms Don's account of his time at Lambourn:

Colin Moyle was our manager at the time, and he knew Don from buying kit at the sports shop. One day they got chatting and Colin asked if Don had considered getting involved with managing a club. When Don said he had thought about it, Colin just asked him to get involved. That was the beginning of it all; we had some great days together – me, Don and Colin – and the club was incredibly successful, particularly in the cup competitions. The day we won the Berks & Bucks Cup was unbelievable. Don said to me afterwards that he had a better journey back after the game with us all having a sing-song on the bus, than he had after the Wembley League Cup final win! The problem with Lambourn was that it was just a football division of a bigger sports club, and there were always tensions, particularly over money.

Listening to Don describe his management days – not just those at Lambourn but also elsewhere – I am struck by just how much he enjoyed his 'second career' in football. Anyone who knows Don will not be surprised that he had such a good time, and made such an impact, at what was, relatively speaking, a low level of football. It is somehow hard to imagine many of today's star players being prepared to coach and manage at such a level; for Don it was ideal – the chance to give something back.

From Lambourn, Don moved on to Swindon Supermarine, also in the Hellenic Premier League, where he led them to the Premier League title. It was a major achievement, but Don's main memory is of a failed FA Vase run: 'I was very disappointed that year because we had a very good side and we should have gone further in the FA Vase than we did. We played Porthleven at home, and we annihilated them, but they equalised with a freak goal in the last minute. Then we lost 2-1 in the replay. I am convinced that had we beaten them we would have gone a long way.'

Despite the success at Supermarine, Don only stayed a season, leaving when it became evident that the club would not be pursuing its application for promotion (to the old Southern League), on financial grounds. Don had no argument with the decision but decided to move on. His next stop would be Hungerford.

We got off to a great start – twelve or thirteen matches unbeaten – and we also had a great run in the FA Cup, where I still say we got a terrible decision, and I am still annoyed thinking about it now. We played Salisbury at Hungerford in the third qualifying round, and one of their players handled the ball on the line. The referee gave us a penalty, but incredibly didn't send the player off. He just booked him, which is against the rules of the game, of course. We should have been 1-0 up against ten men, but they kept all eleven on the pitch and scored with five minutes to go.

We still should have won at Salisbury. We played very well down there – as well as any side I've managed ever did, I think – but we lost 3-2 in the last minute. Salisbury went on to play Hull City in the first round proper of the FA Cup, and I think I would still have been at Hungerford had we got through – things would have just rolled as a result. It was the best side I had. The Supermarine side I had would have run it close, and a number of those players came with me to Hungerford, but the Hungerford team was the best.

The next season was Don's last and he left after a poor start. One game in particular convinced him it was time to go: 'We played at Horsham and you've never seen anything like it. We completely dominated the game: we scored one, missed six. With five minutes to go, our centre half lost the ball on the edge of the area, and it was 1-1. Then, in the last minute, they scored again. Honestly, they hardly had a kick.'

Next stop was Pewsey, in Screwfix Division One – a job which Don describes as being 'in some ways the best of the lot'. When Don joined they were rock bottom, 'something like twelve points adrift' but they then went on a remarkable run.

Looking at the fixtures, I knew we could get out of trouble, because we weren't that bad a side. We won a couple early on, and then from March we won ten of the last twelve and went from bottom to seventh from bottom. We started the run by beating Warminster, who were something like fifth in the table, 7-0 at home. Then, after Warminster, our next five games at home were virtually all against the other sides down at the bottom, in a run, and we won all five. The only game we lost was a Sunday game when I couldn't get a team – we only had twelve in the squad; two people went off injured.

The next season we went over to the Hellenic League and got promoted from the First Division to the Hellenic Premier League at the first attempt. We finished as runners-up. The people at the club then did everything to help. They put up floodlights, which was great, new dugouts, new hard standing round the pitch and everything. Then, I don't know why, people seemed to lose a bit of interest. Results weren't great, which didn't help, and I made a few mistakes. Anyway, I left once then I came back, which was a mistake – I should have stayed away.

At the time, Don commented: 'I had two good years there and I enjoyed myself. The people there are super and I've made a lot of friends. Local football has changed so much since I started out in it in 1992. People wanted to play then, but now it seems like an effort to get them there. I might go back and start watching the Town again now, you never know.'

That was early 2003, and was Don's last involvement on the management side. As far as he's concerned that's it. His weekends now are spent at the chalet in Highcliffe, which Jane and he own.

> I really enjoyed it. Like anything else in life you enjoy it more when things go well, and I had some good times. I met some great people as well. Of course most people knew of me from my Swindon days. It was very competitive – we all used to get carried away a bit – and I'm not sure my family would recognise me as a manager! I had some good days though, particularly at Lambourn, where Clive, Colin and me all got on very well. We went out a lot together, and it was a real sense of community.

There is one other team that Don managed that deserves a mention at this point: Hungerford Veterans. Managed by Don and Colin Moyle, and comprising of players drawn from a variety of backgrounds, with a number of former Swindon Town players (including Jimmy Quinn, Tom Jones and Steve Abbley), this unlikely team gave Don another trip back to Wembley.

It was in 2000, the last year that Wembley staged cup finals, when the Hungerford Veterans reached the final, and played on the hallowed turf before the FA Trophy final between Kingstonian and Kettering. Don really enjoyed it: 'We had a very good side for that competition and, most importantly, we were very fit. I remember we played at Bournemouth and scored seven, and a lot of that was down to fitness. Then we played at Southend and we drew 1-1 before winning on penalties, and I have to say that the referee was shocking. Absolutely dreadful – he gave everything their way. Before we took our spot-kicks I asked him if we would be allowed in the penalty area to take them! I was furious with him.

We did things properly for Wembley. We went and stayed overnight in Watford and had a post-match meal and celebration.

I led the team out with Colin, and the win (they beat a Liverpool side 2-0) was as great a thrill as winning at Wembley with Swindon.

Don, as most people who know him would say, is quite quiet, so how did he cope with management? 'I agree I'm not one to rant and rave; once I've said something, then that's it, as far as I'm concerned – you can't keep going over things. I used to forget half of the things I wanted to say when I got into the dressing room anyway, but I had some good people helping me at all the clubs who said what needed to be said.'

Clive Bettison, basing his opinion on Don's time at Lambourn, would agree:

> Colin Moyle did most of the talking really, but when Don spoke, you listened. It wasn't just because he was someone who had been so successful as a footballer, but it was the way he carried himself as a person – he had just had this aura about him. He wasn't one to rant a lot – he was more like a Sven-Goran Eriksson – but he didn't take any messing around from players and was quite happy to let people go if he thought they were letting him, or the club, down. He was a good coach though. He took training and had a major say on things like set pieces and physical fitness.

So, as he nears his fifty-ninth birthday, Don is content. By the time this book is published he will have parted company with his crutches – a constant companion of his during the early summer – and will be back full-time in his shop, keeping busy but still having time for anyone who wants to come in any talk about his playing days. He still lives in the town in which he made his name, and is a keen follower of both his main two former clubs, as well as football more generally.

The final word should go to Don: 'I've been very lucky really in my life, and I have no complaints. Life has been good to me, and if you'd told me what was going to happen to me when I was a young man leaving Somerset, I wouldn't have believed you. It's been a good life; like everybody I've had ups and downs, but it's the good times that I will always remember.'

Final Reflections

It's the end of June 2004. As I pull up to Don's house, Tim Henman is engaged in another of his epic Centre Court struggles at Wimbledon. He will win this one, but alas not the next one. Don, as always, greets me with a cheery smile. He has been endlessly patient during the writing of the book and, given that we did not know each other before we started, remarkably open and honest. Perhaps tonight the smile is a little broader – this will be the last of our regular chats in the sitting room of his Swindon home.

Tonight is about looking back over his whole career, trying to put all the pieces together to create what the management consultants would call a 'helicopter view'. How, nearly thirty years after it all ended, does Don assess his career?

We begin by talking about the great times. No prize for what the best day was: 'Wembley was the greatest day of my footballing career, there's no doubt about it. When you consider that many players never get the chance to play in a cup final, you realise how fortunate you were. It was brilliant to be able to play there, but to go and win, and to have the chance to score those goals, well…'

Don's voice fades away as he remembers that day in the Wembley mud. It is still the game for which he is best remembered in football, and indeed that final will always be associated with his name, although there are a couple of other games that would run Wembley close.

The Palace 5-0 win over Manchester United was an incredible game. I think it was the best I ever played in a game – particularly as it was in the First Division. That day we played so well, it was incredible; and of course I got a lot of publicity because of the fact that I had a role in all the goals, not just scoring but making them as well. Then the other game would be the 3-3 draw at West Ham in the FA Cup. That was another great day, both for the team and me personally – I suppose it was the first time I'd really played in such a high-profile match as a first-team regular, and to do so well was superb. The only downside was that we didn't win, because we should have done. At least we won in the replay!

How about the great players? Who will Don recall as the best he ever played with?

That's a very difficult one, because I played with some great players over my career. I think though for pure individual talent it would have to be Stan Bowles. He just had so much skill, and when he was focused on his game, he could do anything with a football. Charlie Cooke at Crystal Palace was another great footballer, although I only played with him at the end of his career. Even though he was getting on a bit, you could see what a talent he had: great close control and ability. Then, at Swindon, I was very fortunate to play with some excellent players as well – I'm not going to single anybody out because they're all still my mates and I don't want to upset anyone! Seriously though, that team which won at Wembley was all the better for the fact that it was a team, not individuals, and everybody was a good player. You can see that by the number who went on to play in the First Division, and there were others in that side who could have made the step up but either never got the opportunity, or chose not to.

Those are the easy discussions – great games, great teams, and great players. Now we move on to the more painful memories. What was Don's worst moment in football?

> You've got to say the relegations really because they tarnish the memory of the whole season – they make the season a bad one. I had three relegations in my career, and each one was painful. The one at Swindon was bad, partly because of the way we went down (readers will recall the last day of the season when Swindon and their relegation rivals, Portsmouth, kicked off at different times), but the two relegations at Palace were worse. The one from the First Division was horrible, because we were 'much too good to go down', as they say, and from a personal point of view, having only just got to the First Division – having waited ten years to do so – it was awful to only have six months playing there. Then the second relegation at Palace, well that was just stupid. I still don't really believe that we went straight through that league.

I resist the temptation to ask Don about worst players he played with, although anyone who watched the Swindon Town team in transition in the early 1970s, or the side nearly relegated to the Fourth Division in 1975/76 that Don briefly rejoined, might have a number of candidates. Instead we move on to talk about the one big regret of Don's career – the lack of a full international cap. Would he have traded one for his day at Wembley? Don's response is immediate, and emphatic.

> No, definitely not. The thing is that an international cap is personal really. It's all about one player, whereas Wembley was all about the team, and in fact the whole town. I still meet Swindon people who say it was the best day of their lives. Of course I would have loved to have won a cap, but the team is always more important than the individual, and I wouldn't have taken a day of personal glory ahead of what we did at Wembley. I think I did come close a couple of times to selection, particularly when I was at Palace, but it wasn't to be.

This brings us neatly on to the key area of discussion when anyone considers Don's career. Did he stay at Swindon for too long? His chances of an international cap would surely have been greater, even allowing for Sir Alf Ramsey's suspicion of players of his ilk, had he moved into the First Division earlier?

I think that's true. It would have been a huge gamble for Sir Alf to have picked me when I was at Swindon, although of course I did play for the English League side which he selected, which was as close as I got. So did I stay at Swindon too long? Probably yes, when you look back at it, although do bear in mind that there wasn't much I could do about it. The time I perhaps should have gone was after Wembley, because although we just missed out on promotion the first year in the Second Division, the next two seasons were poor really, and didn't do much for my personal career. But at the time, you don't see it. We all though we would continue to challenge for promotion, and given I was so happy at the club and in the town, as long as I thought I could play in the First Division with Swindon, I wanted to stay. In hindsight, from a purely professional viewpoint, if I could have done, I should have moved earlier. It would have been good to have had more time in the First Division, and when I was a bit younger too… but we'll never know how it would have worked out if I'd left earlier and gone somewhere else. The thing I will always be thankful for is that I had that time at Palace. It was brilliant: the club, the players, the fans, everything.

Our time is up. There is an unspoken contract between Don and I that our sessions will not last too long. Don is still recovering from his latest hip replacement, although there has been a marked improvement in his mobility over the time this book has been written, and he has other things to do – this book has, after all, been written in his free time. I ask him one last question: how would he sum up his career?

It was brilliant overall. I know we've just talked about some of the not-so-good times, but even they were good. If you can't enjoy your life when you are paid to play football, then there's something wrong with you. It's a great life, and the only regret is that it is all over so quickly. I was so fortunate though: overall things went so well, and I've got lots of great memories and made some very good friends through football. I've been very lucky.

This book has been written, as will have been evident, with Don's full co-operation. Yet it is a biography, and not an autobiography. It is therefore time for the biographer to give a view on his subject.

Firstly, what is Don like as a person? Many people reading this may know him personally. They will know what he is like. He is a well-known, and well-liked, figure in Swindon. He is quiet, and in some ways, quite shy, until you get to know him, but he has a great sense of humour, and is excellent company. Others, of course, would know him better than me... here's the view of Alan Whittle.

Don is a great guy, someone who I view as a big mate. He's very generous – generous with his time and always happy to help others. He's a thinker – he doesn't shout or bawl – he's like a sponge: he absorbs everything and then says what he thinks. He never draws much attention to himself. Even after scoring goals all he'd do would be raise his arms and then trot back slowly, as if to say 'I've done my job, what's the fuss!'

Keith Morgan is equally positive about the man: 'Don is a gentleman; a great ambassador for football. He never turns down invitations to present awards. He's a very good businessman too. I know that some of the big sports stores send their people down to see Don, because he can get stuff from the manufacturers that they can't!'

Frank Burrows would agree: 'Don is a quiet, modest bloke, who doesn't say much – although he's got a good brain, and when he speaks he's worth listening to. He's been a good friend, a loyal friend, and he's the type of bloke you'd want to be friends with. He hasn't changed at all since I first met him.'

So, how good was Don? The answer is surely good – very, very good. He was, as the introduction makes clear, surely Swindon Town's greatest ever player, and he showed in one tantalising glimpse in the early 1970s that he had the ability to thrive at the very top level. He would have been in everybody's Fantasy Football team – not only did he score over 150 League goals, but created countless others. A goalscoring winger… there haven't been many of those in the last forty years. Was he international class? At his best, without a doubt. He surely deserved at least one chance to play for his country.

It is noticeable that his one taste of 'international club football', while with Swindon (the matches against Italian sides in the 1969/70 season) was a great success. Also, he was the star of the England youth team when he played for them, and although there is no guarantee that outstanding players at that age go on to make regular full England internationals, he undoubtedly had the talent to play at that level.

So why didn't he become an England regular? Part of it, as we have seen, is the period in which he was at his best. The England manager at that time did not select players of his type. Part of it was also consistency. Don himself would admit that, while at Swindon particularly, he was more effective at home than away. Various others have commented on this fact elsewhere in the book. As he admitted himself when talking about his playing days, there were times when he was riddled by self-doubts. Yet the real reason is overwhelmingly clear. He stayed at Swindon for too long, when one looks at football in isolation.

There are many reasons for this. Don, while keen to do well, is not, as a person, as ruthlessly ambitious as some. For him there were always other considerations than merely what was happening on the pitch. If things off the pitch were going well, then why would he want to move? He has always been someone for whom a sense of belonging is important – whether it be his upbringing in Somerset, or his relationship with the fans, club and town of Swindon. He needed, as a player, to feel secure and appreciated.

Swindon gave him that, and he knew it. I don't think it is any surprise that when he did leave Swindon he went somewhere where he knew the manager, and the manager knew him. There was a level of security for Don that he responded too – he knew he was rated, and therefore had enormous confidence as a result.

Another reason why he stayed is to be found in Don's character. He is a loyal and decent person. Once his transfer requests were turned down, it was not in his nature to create waves until the club was forced to sell him – which, even when contracts were different in the 1960s and '70s, he could have done. He accepted the decision and got on with life.

The last reason why he stayed at Swindon is touched on in the paragraph above. He tried to leave, but the club held the power. He was forced to honour his contract; his career was not really his own. Don would never say it, but with the benefit of hindsight, the club held him back.

Returning to the international scene, I am prepared to stick my neck out and say that had Don left Swindon earlier then he would have been a full international. He would have benefited from playing with top-class players, and his game would have improved as a result. He would have had more publicity (one only has to look at the media coverage when he did eventually step up into the First Division), and would have been more in the public eye. All through his career he was at his best against better opposition – they gave him more space, and Don exploited it. Think of West Ham in 1967, Arsenal in 1969, and Liverpool in 1970: all top-class sides that suffered at the hands of his pace and goalscoring ability.

When should Don have gone? There are probably three possibilities. The first is at the time of the first approach: 1965 from Liverpool. Would that have worked? Possibly Liverpool was a club on the up under the management of Bill Shankly, although not quite the force they later became. The question there is whether Don, at just twenty years of age, would have coped with the pressure on and off the field. Footballing wise, he would have done well, of that I am convinced, but teammates (and to be fair, Don himself), all talk of how quiet Don was as a young man. It might have been too much for the youngster; on the other hand it would have got him into the First Division very early and his prospects of international honours, had he succeeded, would have been high.

Alan Whittle, himself a Liverpudlian, feels that it would have worked out: 'It would have been early for him to have moved, but if anyone could have helped him settle it would have been Shanks, who was great at looking after young players and creating a family feel to a club. Don would have needed to have felt part of a community to have succeeded, because he did need that security, and Liverpool would have given it.'

The second opportunity was the transfer request of 1967, which Swindon turned down. He was then just twenty-two, but was very experienced in League football terms. He had been a first-team regular for three-and-a-half seasons; he was scoring goals regularly and was attracting lots of attention. This might have been a better bet. At that stage he had no idea that Swindon would have such a success-ful season the following year – indeed, one of the triggers for the request was the despondency he felt about the likelihood of the team escaping the Third Division. He would have missed the triumph at Wembley (although without Don it might not have happened) but would have had a chance to test himself against better players week in week out. It could have been a good time to have gone.

With hindsight though, the real missed opportunity was the summer of 1970. He had won the League Cup and then had an outstanding season in the Second Division. He was still only twenty-four. He could have had his choice of clubs. We know that Manchester City, Arsenal, Spurs, Wolves, West Bromwich Albion and Nottingham Forest were interested. He had fulfilled his obligations to Swindon, and more. Yet the club would never sell him – more's the pity from an objective viewpoint.

Instead, Don spent nearly two-and-a-half years playing in a declining team. He would never say it – but his biographer can – they were wasted years. It did him no good, his form undoubtedly suffered and the game of football was deprived the chance to see him at the top level when he was in his prime. Alan Whittle would agree: Don should have left Swindon before he was twenty-five really. He had to show that he could play at the highest level, and that he was good enough to make the step up. I know he would have done well, and it would have set him up for the rest of his career.

When he finally left, in the end, it was too late. Circumstances went against him. Although in some ways, Palace, with the Bert Head connection, was the ideal destination, none of the big clubs would take a chance on him. Don exceeded everybody's expectations, but as the contemporary Palace sources make clear, he was the star man in a relatively poor team, and his goals could not keep them up. It was a glimpse of what might have been. Imagine a younger Don, in a better side. It would have been explosive. By the time he did get back to the top flight with Queens Park Rangers, it really was too late; the hip injury had taken hold, and he wasn't the player of five years previously.

So at one level, the Don Rogers story is one of unfulfilled talent: no international caps, only six months in the top flight of English football when he was at his prime, and three relegations to two promotions (one of which, as it was so early in his career, he barely featured in). Yet that conclusion would be hugely flawed. Yes, he should have played for England. Yes, he could have had a major impact on the First Division playing for a top club, but in the end he will remembered at both Palace and Swindon as one of the most exciting players ever to play for the club. He played a huge part in giving the town of Swindon the best day of its collective life, and within both the SN and SE25 postcodes his name brings genuine affection and a sense of real awe at the way he played his football. He's popular everywhere – nobody I spoke to had a bad word to say about him – and those who remember him as a great player and want to pay homage still regularly visit his sports shop in Swindon. It's not such a bad epitaph really.

Postscript

It's the middle of July. I have been at a function in London and am on the last train back to Swindon, the town where Don made his name. I have some final touches to do to finish the book, and in order to do so have laid out match reports on the table in front of me.

A man walks down towards the buffet past my table. Suddenly, he stops, does a double take, and looks at the report in front of me. 'Don Rogers, Wembley 1969' he says, 'I was there – best day of my life.' He goes on 'What a player – simply superb –the best I've ever seen in a Swindon shirt.'

And with that he's gone. The memory of Don as a player is alive and well.

If you are interested in purchasing
other books published by Tempus, or in case you have
difficulty finding any Tempus books in your local bookshop,
you can also place orders directly through our website

www.tempus-publishing.com